Victory
Over Deception
Through Distinguishing
Between Spirits

By Joyce Gill

ISBN 0-941975-02-9

Revised Edition 1999
© Copyright 1990

**Powerhouse Publishing
PO Box 99
Fawnskin, CA 92333**

Books by A.L. and Joyce Gill

Destined for Dominion
God's Covenant Blessings for You
God's Promises for Your Every Need
Out! In the Name of Jesus

Manuals by the Gills

Authority of the Believer
*How to Quit Losing
and Start Winning*

Church Triumphant
Through the Book of Acts

God's Provision for Healing
*Receiving and Ministering
Gods Healing Power*

The Ministry Gifts
*Apostle, Prophet, Evangelist,
Pastor, Teacher*

Miracle Evangelism
God's Plan to Reach the World

New Creation Image
Knowing Who You Are in Christ

Patterns for Living
From the Old Testament

Praise and Worship
Becoming Worshipers of God

Prayer
Bringing Heaven to Earth

Supernatural Living
Through the Gifts of the Holy Spirit

Table of Contents

Chapter One
Taken by Deception 5

Chapter Two
The Gift That Protects 21

Chapter Three
Areas of Spirit Activity 32

Chapter Four
Distinguishing Between Spirits 43

Chapter Five
Testing a Prophecy 54

Chapter Six
Con-Artists in the Church 62

Chapter Seven
Gullible Christians 72

Chapter Eight
Are We Defenseless? 80

Chapter Nine
This Gift Is for Today 91

Chapter Ten
Responsibilities of Leadership 100

Chapter Eleven
In Conclusion 107

Introduction

Victory Over Deception is a practical, powerful revelation of how we as believers in Jesus Christ can distinguish the spirit behind every situation – how we can avoid Satan's plans to bring death, loss and destruction into our lives.

God has given us marvelous protection from the schemes of Satan, but many of us have remained ignorant of what this protection is. Through the gift of distinguishing between spirits, we can live in victory every day!

But what is this gift? Every time we hear about the gifts of the Holy Spirit, we hear about it. But how many times have we heard anyone teach about what it is?

How do we operate in the gift of distinguishing between spirits?

Angels aren't all in heaven, and demons aren't yet in hell. The spirit world is all around us – angels and demons are all around us. We need this special safeguard, the gift of distinguishing between spirits, that God has provided for believers operating every day in every area of our lives.

Chapter One

Taken by Deception

God Wasn't in the Gold Mine!

I was hurriedly rinsing the dishes and putting them in the dishwasher, when I heard the question, "How much money will it take to fulfill the vision I've given you and A.L.?"

My mind began to do calculations rapidly. "I want you to know," the voice continued, "A.L. is coming home with a lot of money."

I began to consider, What is a lot of money? Hundreds... No. Thousands... No. It will take hundreds of thousands of dollars to fulfill the vision God has given us. Just then, A.L. came through the door carrying a large burlap bag. "What's in the bag?" I asked.

"Gold," he replied.

"Come on, A.L., what's in the bag?"

"Gold," he answered again. "It's gold! Well actually, it's gold ore from a mine in Arizona."

With this "supernatural" beginning, we became involved in one of the most frenzied times we've ever lived through.

A.L. had just met with a lady we knew slightly. She had just returned from a gold mine in Arizona where she had watched them produce gold. She had pictures of gold coming off the shaker table. She had picked up the sample ore

A.L. was carrying, from around the property herself.

The men from Tulsa who were promoting the gold mine stock were wonderful Christian men who were on the boards of several large, well-known ministries. All of these ministries were said to be stockholders in the gold mine, and the story was that God had blessed them so richly that they had decided to sell some of the stock to other, smaller ministries that needed financing.

We were cautious. A friend who is a geologist went to look at the property for us. Yes, there was a mine, and yes, the land certainly looked right for gold. We inquired of the ministries. Yes, these men were on their boards. They seemed to be credible Christian men. We had been praying about finances to reach the world – that was the vision God had given us. And God had said He would supply all our needs according to His riches.

We invested a large amount of our personal money to purchase stock. So did our friends. Soon their friends had invested, and then friends of their friends! We learned later that this was happening to churches and ministries all over the United States.

We were approached again and again by the promoters. They needed this piece of equipment and then the mine would be in regular production. They needed $10,000 for this and $20,000 for that. People kept purchasing more stock. Often we would call the men in Tulsa. They had just uncovered a new strain of gold ore and the assays were fantastic. They would tell us, "God is blessing this operation so much because almost all of the investors are Christians whose motivation is to reach the world with the gospel of Jesus Christ!"

This continued for almost a year and the mine never seemed to make it into full production. Of course, by this time, many of us were getting skeptical. By the end of the next quarter, we could expect to start receiving a return, then it was expected the next quarter, and then the next. After the first stockholders' meeting in Tulsa, we realized something was very wrong. Our concerns grew and so did the concerns of others. A short time later, we learned the company had gone into the first stages of bankruptcy.

At the second meeting of the shareholders, A.L. was voted in as the Chairman of the Board and became involved in an attempt to save the company and the savings of so many Christians who had, like us, invested heavily. At that time, the Official Stockholders List came into our hands. We discovered that only a third of our stock had been registered with the stock transfer house.

As we checked the Stock Register for person after person, the same was true. A small percentage of what they had purchased, or in many cases, none of their stock, was registered. We asked for proofs of purchase from stockholders and we were sent copies of checks which had been deposited in many different accounts. There was no accounting for where most of the millions of dollars had gone. But it seemed very little of the money had actually gone into the mining operation.

There were, or had been, offices in Prescott, Phoenix, and Tulsa. Even as Chairman of the Board, A.L. wasn't able to find company files. He was told that the FBI had confiscated them because of another deal in which one of the men had been involved in the past. He could find no assay reports to support the claims that had been made in promoting the sale of the stock.

A.L. and some of the other stockholders spent a hot summer in Arizona at one of the mines trying to put it into actual production. The first day he was there, he was offered a gold bar "to cover his expenses." He was told, "No one would ever know about it." He refused to make that first compromise.

While he was in Arizona and I was in our home in Houston, I began to spend many extra hours praying about the whole situation. One time, I told A.L. on the telephone, "As I pray in the spirit and ask God how to pray, it's as if my spirit moves all around that mining operation and I can't find enough honesty to even fill a postage stamp."

As he and the others worked, they found this was true. Property that the company was supposed to control wasn't leased. Most of the equipment had been stolen or repossessed. There were no copies of the leases on much of the equipment, and yet, more and more money was demanded to pay "these leases." Equipment, especially the testing equipment, was continuously sabotaged. Threats became an almost daily occurrence. So many "side deals" had been made that even under the most favorable conditions, it would have been impossible to have made a profit. The tailings that were being mined were only a fraction of what they had been represented to be. He could find no truthfulness in the entire operation.

Finally after months had passed, A.L. was able to gain control of the Board of Directors. Then he and the new board discovered for certain that the whole thing was a scam operation. They found receipts showing where the original group of men had purchased gold ore and hired trucks to haul it to the property. This was the ore that was being used to show that the mine was in operation when the potential investors were invited to inspect the mine.

The lady who told us about the mine, along with several others, had walked about the property picking up miscellaneous rock (ore) samples. Then the men on the property had offered to put them into burlap bags and the rock samples were switched to gold ore. It was also discovered that the gold bar which had been held up in the first stockholders' meeting to "prove" the mine was in operation, was produced in another state. The gold in this "sample bar" hadn't come from the mine.

At this time, the new board knew there was no hope for saving the company, and A.L. turned the few records he had been able to gather over to the FBI. The company ended in total bankruptcy and the scam was exposed. Many were indicted and some sentenced to prison.

We spent many hours following this time asking the Lord where we and so many others had gone wrong in hearing from Him.

The "confirmations" we and the others received when we prayed and talked about investing in this gold mine were incredible.

When A.L. came in carrying the gold ore, I was deceived. I believed every word because of the thoughts I had immediately before A.L. told me about the gold mine. I believed they were from God, but I hadn't tested the spirit.

That first night, as A.L. and I discussed this "opportunity," A.L. mentioned that there were two people we should talk to about the gold mine and he named them. The telephone rang immediately and the first man he had named was on the line. We hadn't heard from him in about two months. Even as A.L. began to describe the opportunity to him, the second man called. He had been out of town for the last week and had just returned home. The first man was in gold mining and when he looked at the ore, he was impressed. The second man is a very cautious businessman, and because of him, we did a lot of investigating before we invested. But we didn't spend enough time with God.

A pastor friend of ours was in a small church that had been struggling for existence. Because of medical bills, his personal finances were a disaster, also. His daughter had a dream about her dad and all his financial troubles. In her dream, he was tunneling through the mountain of bills, and suddenly struck gold. She called him in the morning. "Dad," she said, "Your financial problems are taken care of! God showed me last night that you are going to strike gold and it will take care of all the bills." That day he heard about the gold mine stock being made available to small ministries. Because of the "confirmation" of his daughter's dream, he took the very little he and his wife had in retirement savings and purchased every bit of stock he could.

People would be talking about buying this stock and a scripture reference would suddenly pop into their minds. To some, the reference was to hidden riches. I will give you the treasures of darkness, riches stored in secret places, so that you may know that I am the Lord, the God of Israel, who summons you by name (Isaiah 45:3).

When A.L. came into a position of leadership, we heard many devastating stories of what had happened in the lives of investors. A young couple had sold their home and put all of the money from the proceeds into the gold stock.

They were assured they could easily get their investment out in time to purchase another house before two years had passed. They lost their first home, the money from selling that home, and then they were forced to pay capital gains tax on the proceeds of that sale since they weren't able to purchase another home within the government's allowable time of two years.

An elderly man, who had worked as an administrator for a large ministry for many years, took all of his life's savings, invested it, and lost it. Even though he was over the age of seventy, he had to find a new job and begin working again. Some of the "wonderful Christian men" who knew this was a swindle, sold him the stock. He had thought they were his personal friends.

All over the United States, committed Spirit-filled Christians invested millions of dollars into a scam operation. We've even met missionaries in other countries who've purchased this stock.

Why? The web of deceit of this scam operation was planned in brilliant detail. The man who set it up knew what he was doing. We've been told that he has a long history of scam operations. He was able to involve key Christian leaders, and then get them to compromise their Christian principles. These men gave the operation the "credibility" it needed. Perhaps these Christian men started out being deceived themselves. We've been told that they had lost a great deal of money in a previous scam operation with this same man. When they knew the truth, however, they became part of the new scheme in an attempt to recover their losses. Then the scam grew as each person trusted the word and discernment of others.

When we learned the truth, it was shocking to realize the number of lies that had been told by people who claimed to be Christians. Not half truths, not social lies, but lies meant to deceive and defraud. All of the money these men took did them no good. The money they received from their plan of deceit could never buy them happiness or peace with God. They declared bankruptcy in the following years and we understand have plead guilty and been sentenced for their crimes.

God has revealed many things to us since that time. The fact we believed it was God who told us to get involved with the mining operation didn't force God to make all those beliefs come to pass. We thought our faith was in what God had said, but we had been listening to a different spirit.

A.L. and I were forced to sell our large home. The house and the money were just "things" and we've done without them. However, the hardest part for us to accept was the way we had missed God and been deceived! Now, years later, we know the reason this could happen. Again and again, we trusted others rather than testing the spirits behind the scene for ourselves. We were deceived, manipulated, controlled and defrauded by the enticing words of men and by the demon spirits of deception operating through them. God had provided the gift of distinguishing between spirits. We had the gift of distinguishing between spirits residing within us, but we had neglected to operate in that gift.

During this same time, A.L. and I would be talking in our home about something and someone would call from across town with "a word from the Lord" to confirm that conversation.

Angels are not all in heaven, and demons are not yet in hell. The spirit world is around us. Angels and demons are all around us.

We were being attacked by familiar spirits and by spirits of deception, and we weren't operating in our God-given gift of distinguishing between spirits. The demons that heard our conversations would go immediately to someone else and have them call and give us "a message from God." We never tested the spirit behind these "confirmations." They were supernatural, and we just accepted them as from the Lord.

Even close to the end, when we were working with the attorney in an attempt to save the company, the spirits of deception were at work. Since there was very little money, and at that time, we believed there was a slight possibility that the company could be turned into a profitable operation, the attorney accepted the mining stock as part of his payment. One evening, he went to a charismatic prayer group and a woman walked up to him who knew nothing about the company or about what he was doing for it.

She said, "I know this sounds strange, but I want you to know that as you and your wife walked into the room, I saw you carrying buckets of gold. I don't mean money. I saw buckets and buckets of gold. You are going to be extremely wealthy because of some connection you now have with gold." From what we know now, we wonder if the message God intended was, "You are carrying visions of buckets and buckets of gold. Lay aside these thoughts and put your whole attention on Me." Or perhaps, she was just prophesying from the wrong spirit.

Jesus said that in the last days, the days would be shortened less even the very elect be deceived (Matthew 24). We are in those days. The elect have been, and are being, deceived by the Father of Lies.

We must begin to walk in the supernatural every day, in every situation. We must begin to test every message we believe to be from God. We must test every sermon we hear. We must test every appeal for money we receive. Is it from God? Does it promote the person giving the message? Does it promote our own self-interest? Does it agree exactly with what the Bible says?

Our protection from the deceit of the con-artists in the church and in the business world is in the operation of the revelation gifts of the Holy Spirit. As we learn more and more of His Word, and as we spend more time worshiping Him, we will discern the evil spirits that are around us and be able to stand against them.

Following this time of deception, A.L. and I spent weeks, months and even years studying the gift of distinguishing between spirits. How had we and hundreds of other Spirit-filled, committed Christians been so deceived? How could we protect ourselves in the future? How could others protect themselves?

We asked God to reveal to us the "steps to knowing deception" so that something good could come from this experience. We never did receive the steps we were looking for since there are no simple rules to cover this area. God did tell us that as we spend more and more time with Him, we would instantly know an "alien" presence, and that we would operate more and more in the spiritual gift of distinguishing between spirits.

The writer of the book of Hebrews speaks of the mature believers and how they learned to distinguish good from evil. **But solid food is for the mature, who by constant use have trained themselves to distinguish good from evil (Hebrews 5:14).** Notice that it says by constant use; they trained themselves.

We, and hundreds like us, hadn't trained ourselves to distinguish good from evil. We hadn't learned to know in our spirits when we came into contact with deception.

What Is Deception?

The first step to staying out of deception is understanding what deception is.

One morning as I was waking up, my eyes were still closed and I saw lines everywhere as if on a large sheet. The lines were at all different slants and lengths. But there was one line through the center and it was perfectly straight from the top to the bottom and I knew this line represented God.

When builders need a line that is absolutely perpendicular, they use a plumb line. A plumb line is a cord with a heavy weight at the bottom of it. That weight, working by the law of gravity, will pull the line straight down. It's never confused by what's around it. It doesn't try to conform to door casings or corners, or any other lines that might appear to be straight.

Amos told us about a perfect plumb line. The Lord was standing by a wall that had been built true to plumb, with a plumb line in his hand. And the Lord asked me, 'What do you see, Amos?'

'A plumb line,' I replied.

Then the Lord said, 'Look, I am setting a plumb line among my people Israel; I will spare them no longer' (Amos 7:7b,8).

Today, Jesus is our plumb line. To know what is good or evil, what is right or wrong, we must measure it against the life and teachings of Jesus and the revelation of God's Word.

Deception is anything that is just a little off from the truth. Satan doesn't come to us with something that is so far from the truth we will recognize it immediately. He knows if he tried to feed us a pail of garbage, we would refuse it. So he feeds us something enticing that is just a little off from the truth. Remember how he asked Eve some questions in the Garden of Eden that sounded similar to what God had said? He used the words of God, but he misquoted them slightly – just enough to deceive without the error being recognized by Eve.

If we take two lines and one is straight and the other is off just two or three degrees, as we extend those lines, they become further and further apart. Deception may be believing something that has just a little error, but if that error isn't corrected, it will progressively lead us further from God. Accepting that little error makes us more and more vulnerable to other areas of deception.

Sometimes the deception is simple, with only a minor error, or it may be, as in the Arizona gold mine, a deception that is carefully set up in minute detail.

A Little Error Brings Death

Recently, we ministered to a former minister from a certain denomination who had had cancer throughout his whole body. About a year before, this man had been totally healed of throat cancer. He was tested following that healing and his healing had been confirmed.

Later, he was in a service and the person in charge said, "There is a minister here from a certain denomination who has cancer of the throat. Would you stand up?" Our friend wanted to know what God had to say to him, so he jumped up immediately. That quickly, he accepted back the cancer.

The words that came forth were in error. The words were "There is a certain minister... who has cancer." He had been a minister with a certain denomination and he had cancer in the past. That is deceiving! I wonder myself if I would have been wise enough not to have stood.

By standing up, he received back the hurts and rejections that had come to him as he had resigned from his church and denomination. All the harsh words, all the pain of the separation, all the hurts – the cancer was back. Often cancer can come upon a person going through a terrible time of emotional ordeal. When we met with him a few months after that meeting, the cancer had spread throughout his entire body.

As we prayed and received revelation through the distinguishing between spirits, we knew in the spirit that right in the center of his being there was a dreadful mass, evil, tangled, ugly, black strings. The strings from that mass were going throughout his entire body. We didn't know if what we "saw" was physical or spiritual. It didn't matter. We knew it was the center of the cancer.

A nurse was standing near us as we put our hands where the mass was and she said immediately, "That's the spleen." She continued, "Medical science is now realizing that bitterness often settles in the spleen." All the bitterness of leaving the denomination, of leaving his friends, or having them turn on him, had settled into his spleen. Through distinguishing between spirits, we knew that and we were able to minister at the source of the problem. Once again, he was totally healed. We warned him that he would need to keep himself from being pulled back into painful disputes with former friends from that denomination.

Paul wrote, It is for freedom that Christ has set us free. Stand firm, then, and do not let yourselves be burdened again by a yoke of slavery (Galatians 5:1).

Chapter Two

The Gift That Protects

Now, let me go back to the year we received the baptism in the Holy Spirit – back to when the spiritual gift of distinguishing between spirits, along with the other gifts of the Holy Spirit, first began to operate in our lives – back to the time we did know which spirit was speaking – back before we had, in ignorance, let the gift of distinguishing between spirits slip from our lives.

Death Stalked the Road

We were coming down a steep mountain road about six o'clock one Sunday morning on our way to church. It was dark and the road was deserted. I began to feel an immense evil surround me. I felt as though I couldn't move. I could hardly breathe. As the feeling of evil grew stronger and stronger, I continued to pray about it. I began to understand what was happening in the spirit realm.

I said to A.L. as he was driving, "A.L., there is evil on the road. I've been praying about it and I know it's a car without lights. I don't know if it's in our lane, coming toward us, or on the side of the road. I just know it's terribly dangerous." Even as I spoke those words, I felt foolish. What if it was my imagination? What if nothing was wrong and I was causing fear needlessly?

A.L.'s foot hit the brake and he slowed down more and more as we drove around curve after curve. The feeling of danger had become almost suffocating. We came around another curve, to a slightly straighter place in the road and a man was standing in our lane waving both arms above his head trying to get us to stop. His car was stopped on the right shoulder of the road with its lights out just as I had said.

Instead of stopping to help as he would normally have done, A.L. knew this was the evil I had been speaking about. He pushed the accelerator all the way down, jerked the car abruptly into the other lane and careened past the man. Instantly, the feeling of danger left.

Later, we learned a couple of Christian young men had stopped to help someone in the early morning hours in about the same place on that road. Days later, their bodies were found in a nearby desert. Satan had come to rob, steal and destroy.

God's will wasn't that they be killed. They were His children. They had the same Holy Spirit we had. What was the difference? We had listened to the Spirit. We had heeded His warnings.

Distinguishing Between Spirits Is...

A.L. and I received the baptism in the Holy Spirit in September of 1972. Since then we've attended hundreds of seminars, conferences, special meetings and regular services. From that time until now, we've never heard anyone teach on the gift of distinguishing between spirits in any detail. This must be the most misunderstood and ignored gift of the Holy Spirit. And yet we're coming into a time when if we don't know the spirit we're hearing from, we're going to be confused, hurt, deceived and even destroyed.

Satan doesn't want us to know about this gift. Our ignorance has given him free reign in our lives, our businesses and our churches. Satan has been able to do almost anything to us because we don't understand how to distinguish between spirits. Often we don't know who is talking to us and as a result, we react from reasoning and emotion based on a false word, rather than on the Word of God.

The apostle Paul wrote, **To one there is given through the Spirit the message of wisdom, to another the message of knowledge by means of the same Spirit, to another faith by the same Spirit, to another gifts of healing by that one Spirit, to another miraculous powers, to another prophecy, to another distinguishing between spirits, to another speaking in different kinds of tongues, and to still another the interpretation of tongues** (1 Corinthians 12:8-10).

Flowing in the Gifts of the Holy Spirit

The *King James Bible* calls this gift "the discerning of spirits." *The New International Version* uses the words, "distinguishing between spirits." It does seem better to call this gift of the Holy Spirit the distinguishing between spirits since the word "discernment" has a lot of wrong implications.

Discernment is a human ability. If we walked into a friend's house and her eyes were red, we could tell she had been crying. If we noticed the bills and her checkbook open on the desk, it wouldn't take much discernment to know that she was having financial difficulties.

Discernment is in the area of the mind – in the area of the soul. It's not of the spirit. It's not wrong. It's simply not in the supernatural realm of the Holy Spirit. Anyone can operate in discernment. They don't need a relationship with the Holy Spirit to do so. It's a natural ability of the human soul.

Distinguishing between spirits happens in our spirits. It's in our spirits that we know what God is saying. It's the Spirit of God bringing revelation to our spirits.

There has been teaching that each person is to operate in just one of the gifts of the Holy Spirit. However, I believe the Scriptures teach that all the gifts of the Holy Spirit are to operate in all believers at various times. Many times a person will learn to flow in certain gifts more than others, but all the gifts are resident in each believer after being baptized in the Holy Spirit.

If God wants to speak to us, or through us to a group, He uses the vocal gifts of the Holy Spirit – tongues, interpretation, or prophecy. If He wants to reveal something to us, or through us, He uses distinguishing between spirits, the word of knowledge or the word of wisdom.

As all the gifts of the Holy Spirit operate in our lives, they mingle and flow together. When we operate in distinguishing between spirits, we may know that something is evil. The word of knowledge may inform us about the location or source of that evil. Then the word of wisdom can tell us what to do with that knowledge.

Traveling down the road, God gave me the gift of distinguishing between spirits when I felt such evil and then knew there was a terribly dangerous spirit ahead of us on the road. As I prayed, I knew it involved a car with its lights turned off. That was a word of knowledge. When A.L. saw the man in the road, God gave him a word of wisdom. Instead of slowing down to decide what to do, he knew in his spirit to accelerate rapidly, swerving the car violently to keep the man from his plan of action.

The gift of distinguishing between spirits is a supernatural insight into the realm of the spirit world. It reveals the type of spirit, or spirits, behind a person, an action or a message. It's a knowing in your spirit that comes by supernatural revelation about the source, nature, and activity of any spirit. It may come as a voice, a thought, an impression, a vision or a dream.

It's not the gift of discernment. We may hear people say, "I have the gift of discernment," but there is no gift of discernment. They either have the gift of discerning or distinguishing between spirits or they are operating in the human ability of discernment. Remember, one is of the spirit, the other is of the soul, or mental area.

Distinguishing between spirits isn't mind reading, mental penetration, or psychological insight. It's not being critical or judging, and it's not identifying character faults in someone else. These are soul areas, areas of the mind, or of mental sensitivity to others.

Some people find it hard to learn to move in the spirit realm because they see and operate in the natural realm all the time. Many people operate in areas of the intellect. They want everything to be logical, everything to be where they can study it, analyze it and understand it. The spirit realm isn't that way.

"Something Told Me..."

The gifts of the Holy Spirit are not mystical or difficult to understand. Every Spirit-filled Christian has operated in the gifts of the Holy Spirit, but perhaps due to lack of knowledge, hasn't recognized it at the time.

People say, "Oh, something told me..." We stop them right there if we know they are Christians. "Who told you? What is 'something'?" They usually look somewhat puzzled and say, "God, maybe...?"

We must acknowledge the power of God at work within ourselves. We should boldly say, "The Spirit of God told me..." As we begin to do this, we will release the Holy Spirit to tell us more.

It may seem safer to say, "Something told me..." However, when we do that, we aren't acknowledging our relationship with God. We cannot do that and become skilled in moving in the gifts of the Holy Spirit. Many Spirit-filled believers have operated in distinguishing between spirits, but haven't recognized what was happening. It's good to ask the Lord to bring the times to remembrance when He has revealed something to us through the spiritual gift of the distinguishing between spirits. As we recognize how God has worked in the past, our faith grows in that area and we will allow Him to operate more in the future.

If you desire to operate more in the spiritual gift of distinguishing between spirits, pray this prayer with me.

Father,

I ask You now to reveal to me those times when You have operated through me in the gift of distinguishing between spirits and I haven't realized it. Let me understand that You have already shown me many things. Lead me to an awareness of them.

Right now, I ask that You open my understanding to those things that have happened in my own life so that as I am reading these examples, I will know when You have already spoken to me in this way! I ask this in the name of Jesus!

Thank You, Lord!

Now, consciously open your spirit to understand things that have happened in your own life. If you have received the baptism of the Holy Spirit, you have been operating in the discerning of spirits even though you may have been unaware of it.

God Warned Him Twice

An example of this happened when a friend of ours went shopping about ten o'clock one night. He had two young children and his wife had just discovered they were out of milk. He took their oldest son with him and drove to a neighborhood store. There were no other cars in the parking lot, and as he parked by the door, he noticed two men leaning against the wall. He had the impression that they were "not up to any good." He got out of the car, picked up his son, walked into the store, and purchased the milk. Before he came out of the store, he saw the same men and knew, "Those two evil men are still there".

He walked past them to his car, leaned over to put his son in the infant seat and climbed in himself. Just as he started to close the door, he saw a gun pointed directly at his face. The man demanded his money, he argued, and in the scuffle was shot through the knee.

In the hospital, he looked up at A.L. and said, "How could I have been so stupid? God warned me twice and I still walked right out there!"

He had been so intent on purchasing the milk, on carrying out his own plans, that he hadn't taken time to listen to God. Our friend had ignored God's warnings. "Something told him those men were evil." What if he had trained himself to recognize the voice of God? What if he had stopped saying, "Something told me." What if he had started to listen to the "still small voice" within himself before this happened?

That is distinguishing between spirits. He knew the spirits of those men before he parked his car, but he hadn't trained himself to be aware when the gift of distinguishing between spirits was operating.

An Angel or a Human Spirit?

When we begin to be aware of distinguishing between spirits, there is a danger that we might center our attention only on the evil things around us. We can also distinguish the presence of God.

Have you ever heard the leader in a meeting say, "The presence of God is here to heal the sick"? Or someone might say, "God wants us to lift our hands and praise Him." They are distinguishing the different moves, or anointings of the Holy Spirit.

When I was a teen-ager, I occasionally traveled from Texas to Kentucky by train. I would make several transfers between trains and I was always apprehensive about changing from one train to the next. I was especially anxious when I needed to take a cab and go from one station to another in a strange city.

One time, I found a cab and went to the next station, but this time, my tickets were written incorrectly and I wasn't supposed to change stations. By the time I returned to the first station, I had missed my train. It was twelve hours until the next train left and I was forced to spend the night in the train station. To get away from some evil men, I spent the last six hours in the ladies room.

When it was close to the time my train was due, I knew I had to go into the main part of the station and find where to board the train, but I was really panicky. I was afraid the men would still be there. I was certain I would miss the next train. However, finally, I forced myself to go out where I could hear trains being announced.

It was a huge station and I sat down in the waiting area on a seat at the end of the row. By then I was afraid to have any man near me. However, an older man walked purposely over and sat down right next to me. When he did, I was instantly full of peace. One minute I was terrified, the next minute I was at peace. It was like a blanket of peace surrounded that man and as he sat down it surrounded me also. I felt it almost as tangible as a blanket.

I've no idea what the man knew. I don't know what God told him. As he sat down, he said, "Good morning." My answer, if any, was very brief. He turned to me and said, "You know the Houston train will be on track eight. I'm leaving later on the train to Florida." Why did he tell me where my train would soon be? How did he know which train I was taking? Why did he let me know he wasn't going to be on the train with me – that I didn't need to be afraid of him? Why did he sit there with me until my train was called and I left to board it?

Perhaps, the man was an angel. Maybe, and to me this possibility is more exciting, it was a human spirit, so attuned to God that my heavenly Father could send him through a large train station to one terrified girl to bring her peace.

When we operate in distinguishing between spirits, it's important to realize we can distinguish good spirits as well as evil.

Chapter Three

Areas of Spirit Activity

Good ~ Evil ~ Or Human?

We can distinguish spirits from three distinct categories – good, evil and human. For many years, I thought there were only two. I thought there was only good and evil. Everything was either black or white. I didn't understand anything in between. Then I learned that there were three categories.

There are three sources of spirit activity – God, Satan and human. There is the Spirit of God. Often, we have the concept of God being in a far away heaven and so we think of the heavenly spirit realm as being far from us. However, the spirit realm of God is all around us. When we accept Christ, He comes into us, doesn't He? Christ is in us and we are in Him.

The writer of the book of Acts expressed this when he wrote, **God did this so that men would seek him and perhaps reach out for him and find him, though he is not far from each one of us. 'For in him we live and move and have our being' (Acts 17:27,28b).**

This realm includes the Spirit of God – the Father, Son and Holy Spirit – all the good angels, and other heavenly beings.

When Christians come together, we don't need to operate in distinguishing between spirits to know God is there. In Matthew we're told that,

Where two or three come together in my name, there am I with them (Matthew 18:20).

We accept His promise as true. Sometimes, we're more aware of His presence than at other times, but He is always there because His Word says He is.

The other area of spirit activity that I saw so clearly was satanic. I thought something was either of God or it was of the devil. The satanic realm includes the devil and all the demons. I used to think demons were off in some primitive land and Satan was somewhere up in the atmosphere. This is not true. Demon spirits are in all parts of the world. The apostle Peter made it clear that Satan is around us when he wrote, **Be self-controlled and alert. Your enemy the devil prowls around like a roaring lion looking for someone to devour. Resist him, standing firm in the faith (1 Peter 5:8,9b).**

The third area of spirit activity is the human spirit. When you begin to operate in distinguishing between spirits, you will begin to distinguish the nature of a person's human spirit or other spirits. Many times I will have a conversation with a person and I will be talking to A.L. about it later. He will ask, "Which person was that?" Then I realize I don't know how to describe the person physically. Instead of noticing the person's physical appearance, I was feeling the nature of their spirit.

In responding to the needs of people, we must become more aware and sensitive to the spirit of that person than we are to the outward appearance. With this sensitivity, we can be much more effective. We will respond to the root cause of a problem and not just to the outward symptoms.

One time A.L. and I were shopping in a store in Los Angeles. We wanted to purchase a rather expensive item to match the one we had at home. We went into the proper department, found the stock number for that item, and approached a lady working in that department. We said that we would like to purchase this item and gave her the stock number. She refused to get it for us. We waited for awhile thinking she was busy, but we didn't see any other customers around. Finally, we went back and said, "You know, we're still waiting for that item." She still wouldn't go after it for us. We waited about half an hour and finally we went back again the third time. Very unwillingly, she left to find it, but even then she didn't bring it to us. We found it on a cart in another aisle of that department. What should have taken us about ten minutes, took almost an hour.

As we walked through the store to the check-out counter, we saw the manager standing in the aisle and told him what had happened. We continued, "She's costing your store sales! We wanted this one to match the one we have at home, or we never would have stayed to purchase it here."

He looked at us and asked, "Was she a black lady?"

I realized I didn't know. I looked at A.L. and asked him, "Was she black?"

He couldn't remember either. Finally, after thinking, he replied, "I don't know. Well, maybe... Oh, I remember, her badge said she was the department manager." We both had been struck by her spirit. Neither of us had even noticed the color of her skin. Instead, we noticed how the evil spirits within her were reacting to the Spirit of God within us.

Paul explained this when he wrote, For our struggle is not against flesh and blood, but against the rulers, against the authorities, against the powers of this dark world and against the spiritual forces of evil in the heavenly realms (Ephesians 6:12).

Mixture Is Not Good

Jesus taught about the mixture of good and evil when He gave us the parables of the kingdom. He told us that wheat and tares were growing together and that they would remain together until the end times. He also taught about mixture when He gave us the parable of the net and fish.

Once again, the kingdom of heaven is like a net that was let down into the lake and caught all kinds of fish. When it was full, the fishermen pulled it up on the shore. Then they sat down and collected the good fish in baskets, but threw the bad away. This is how it will be at the end of the age. The angels will come and separate the wicked from the righteous and throw them into the fiery furnace, where there will be weeping and gnashing of teeth (Matthew 13:47-51).

We've always considered this parable to refer to the saved and unsaved and it does. It's interesting that the saved and unsaved look so much alike it takes the angels to tell them apart.

John knew there would be mixture when he warned us to test the spirits. Dear friends, do not believe every spirit, but test the spirits to see whether they are from God, because many false prophets have gone out into the world. This is how you can recognize the Spirit of God: Every spirit that acknowledges that Jesus Christ has come in the flesh is from God, but every spirit that does not acknowledge Jesus is not from God. This is the spirit of the antichrist, which you have heard is coming and even now is already in the world (1 John 4:1-3).

John wasn't talking about a spirit that was going to meander up to us in a flowing, transparent type of garment – like Casper the friendly ghost. A spirit is going to come to us in the form or body of other humans. It's going to speak to us through a human voice. That is the reason we're warned of false prophets in this passage. False prophets operate in and around our churches and Bible studies.

When I first received the baptism of the Holy Spirit, I operated in a clear gift of distinguishing between spirits, but I didn't know what it was. A.L. and I knew nothing about any of the gifts of the Holy Spirit. I remember leaving charismatic services saying, "A.L., I thought that when so and so gave a prophecy it was from God until she said..." Or I would say I didn't think a particular message was really from God.

A.L. became concerned. He said, "Joyce, I've never known you to be so critical. You can't let this become part of your life." Through ignorance of the spiritual gifts, we began to limit the Holy Spirit's operation in the area of distinguishing between spirits.

When this happens, we are susceptible to what we call mixture. Often there is a mixture of spirits in connection with a meeting, a minister or a ministry. Some of it's from God, some is from the human spirit and some is from Satan or evil spirits. Different spirits are in control at different times and this can be confusing.

When we became involved with established ministries, we felt they knew so much more than we, that we allowed our own "knowing" from the Lord to be lost in what we were hearing them say. We thought, "He's the pastor, so what he says or does must be right." If there was a question in our minds, we assumed we were wrong.

We went through much self-doubt and deception because we didn't understand the gift of distinguishing between spirits. We didn't understand we were to judge every prophecy before God. Finally, we came to the place where we couldn't tell if a person, a message or a situation was actually from God or not.

37

One time a friend of ours was sitting with us in a service and about the middle of the service, he whispered, "I can't stand this mixture. I'll meet you outside later." He left. We remained in the meeting trying to figure out what he was talking about. We thought the service was great!

I wish we had asked him more definite questions after that service. It might have saved us from some real problems in our own life! He was a man who spent hours alone studying his Bible, talking to God and listening to Him. Those well-spent hours had become a protection surrounding him. His spirit was so tuned to God that he immediately distinguished that there wasn't a purity of God's Spirit operating in that meeting.

We went from one position of mixture to another listening to the words of men instead of the Spirit of God. We hadn't really heard the words found in Job. Hear my words, you wise men; listen to me, you men of learning. For the ear tests words as the tongue tastes food. Let us discern for ourselves what is right; let us learn together what is good (Job 34:2-4).

Notice that we're to discern for ourselves what is right and good.

God Gives Us a Choice

The time came when God started showing me the "behind the scenes" complexion of the church we were involved in. I remember I was driving down the freeway and it was as if an understanding of the whole situation started to come to me. I said, "God, I don't want to know it!" I will never forget that evening as I actually said out loud in the car, "God, I shut the door. I don't want to know any more about peoples' lives and motives."

We had been so hurt by "Christians" and ministries that I felt I couldn't handle knowing anything more. I wanted to remain in peaceful ignorance and think everyone was walking purely before the Lord. Because I chose not to listen to God's warning, A.L. and I were hurt badly by things that happened later in that church. Perhaps if I had listened, God would have led us in the spirit to combat the powers of Satan in that situation. Maybe He would have led us out earlier. We can never know that now.

You might ask, "What do you mean when you say, 'I closed the door?'" God doesn't force Himself, or His knowledge on any of us. I made a decision that day to stop the operation of the distinguishing between spirits in my life. I closed the door to that knowledge in my inner spirit by an act of my own will.

As a result of my closing the door that night, we did become deceived by the gold mine scam that cost us thousands of dollars. We didn't operate in distinguishing between spirits, but listened instead to the promising words of men.

How to Flow in This Gift

If we want to distinguish between spirits consistently, we must spend time with God. We must spend time studying His Word. We must avoid compromise and deception which will open the door for "mixture" to come into our lives and ministries.

We hear a lot of mixture on Christian television, and it's a good place to learn how to operate in distinguishing between spirits. Open your spirit as you listen to each program. Ask God to let you operate in distinguishing between spirits as you watch.

Have you ever watched programs selling some type of real estate course? They tell you for thirty minutes how you can "make a killing in real estate" if you will just purchase their course and learn how. Some "Christian" speakers operate in the same type of spirits. They are spirits of greed – "get rich quick without working" spirits. You can also distinguish controlling spirits, spirits of deception, and self-exalting spirits in various programs.

As you pray in this area, God will lead you to sincere men of God, as well. The surprising thing is that you may, or may not, agree with them doctrinally, but you will know who they are before God. These are the ministries to pray for, and as God leads, to support.

Years ago, I watched and listened to a large television ministry and I felt in my spirit it was like a cancerous growth on the body of Christ. They would plead for more money for this or that project. They were operating in controlling spirits and in spirits of self-gratification. They would say, "If God doesn't provide our needs, this ministry will close."

I would pray, "O God, let it close. That will stop the drain on Christian finances." Many of our friends gave heavily to this ministry and for a time I identified with John the Baptist as a "voice crying in the wilderness." Now the ministry has fallen and the world has enjoyed bringing reproach on the name of Jesus as a result. How much better it would have been if God's people, individually, had operated in His gift of distinguishing between spirits and had withheld their offerings, bringing a natural death to that deception.

In the past, as you were involved in some ministries, did you feel within yourself there was something wrong? Did you argue with that "impression" saying, "Oh no, look how big they are. Look at how many people they're reaching. Look at this... look at that... look at the other...." You ignored what the Holy Spirit was telling you. You reasoned away the voice of God. You may have given money to them. Then when the truth was exposed, you felt betrayed. Much of what they said and did was true, but they had wrong motives – wrong spirits. That is mixture. You listened to the enticing words of men instead of the Spirit of God. You were controlled and manipulated and now you are hurt, confused, angry, and fearful.

When these things happen to us, there are several things that we must do to bring peace back into our lives. First, we must honestly acknowledge what has happened. Then we must forgive the persons involved and begin to pray for them. We must forgive ourselves for being deceived. Then over a period of time, we should ask the Lord to explain to us where we entered into deception. What door was open in our lives that we didn't hear Him more clearly?

Every Christian is responsible for himself. God has given each of us the gift of distinguishing between spirits for our protection. Each of us can "know" in the Lord, the spirits of those who labor among us. Before we receive from a person, we must recognize which spirit they are operating in.

The apostle Paul wrote, **And we beseech you, brethren, to know them which labor among you, and are over you in the Lord and admonish you; And to esteem them very highly in love for their work's sake (1 Thessalonians 5:12,13a KJV).**

If we remain in the mixture places, we will not be able to operate clearly in distinguishing between spirits. If we don't walk in total forgiveness, we will not be able to operate freely in the gifts of the Holy Spirit.

The choice is ours. Deuteronomy 30:19 says, **This day I call heaven and earth as witnesses against you that I have set before you life and death, blessings and curses. Now choose life, so that you and your children may live.**

Chapter Four

Distinguishing Between Spirits

A Flicker of Danger

The Holy Spirit usually doesn't knock us over the head to get our attention. It might be easier if He did! If someone comes up and taps us on the shoulder, we know it. In comparison, the Holy Spirit barely presses our garment. He usually speaks to us in a still, small voice or by a slight impression. We must learn to be sensitive to His warnings and directions.

We live in the mountains now, and one day I was driving down our steep mountain road with its many curves. We were in a hurry to be somewhere on time. I felt just a flicker of an impression in my spirit. I hurried on around the next curve or two and then I thought, You're being stupid, Joyce. The Holy Spirit is saying something to you and you're more intent on getting to your destination. I pulled the car off the road and stopped. In my spirit, I was still racing down the road. So, I took the keys out of the ignition and dropped them in my lap. I made a decision to stop completely so that I could hear from the Lord.

A.L. looked at me and asked, "What's going on?"

I replied, "The Holy Spirit said something to me, but I don't know what it was. I didn't understand it. It was a flicker. But we're not going around another curve until we know what the Holy Spirit said."

We didn't move the car until we knew what the danger was. We began to pray until our spirits became quiet and in communion with God. Then He showed us through a word of knowledge the whole planned incident. We went into warfare and bound it from happening. This time, the danger didn't involve us, but one of our children. Satan had a plan to take his or her life through a head-on collision on that road.

Can we prove that? No. God showed us the devil's plan, and we came against it in the spirit and it didn't happen! Praise God!

You may ask, "What is a flicker?" I'm sure you've experienced it yourself. It comes as a slight impression. There must have been times when you were trying to remember someone's name and it almost came to you, but you couldn't quite catch it. Or you were trying to remember the name of a place and it was right there in your mind, but you couldn't quite grasp what it was. The impression lasts for only a second or two. Usually, we don't grasp the name or place because we're trying so hard to remember it. We are too tense. Then later, when we no longer need the information, it will flash into our minds.

In the spirit realm, we may not receive a message because we're too involved with the physical realm in which we live. Then, when we feel a flicker in our spirit, we must stop what we're doing and move into the spirit area. A.L. and I didn't learn this lesson easily.

Years ago, when our youngest daughter was about fifteen, I drove a Toyota Cressida. We were preparing to leave on a short trip the next morning and I had hurried out in that car to run some errands. I was rushing home and just about to enter the freeway, when I felt a flicker of danger ahead. I pulled into a side area and stopped the car. This is what I prayed, "Father, if I'm going to be in an accident on the freeway, I'm not going on the freeway! Show me what to do." I sat there for several minutes. Then, in my spirit, I felt an almost reluctant permission to go on the freeway, that I wasn't going to be in an accident. I entered the freeway and drove carefully home.

As I parked the car in front of the house, I thought, I wonder what that impression was about before I entered the freeway. I wondered, but I didn't spend time with the Lord to find out!

The next morning, we left on the trip. The following day our daughter was in a terrible accident in that Toyota. Her boyfriend had decided to take the car for a ride and she went with him. It was raining and they went around a nearby corner too fast. He lost control of the car and they hit a light pole. Both of them went through the windshield. Cindy went through a lot of pain, and for several years she was attacked continuously by fear when riding in a car. My car was destroyed.

Why? Because I hadn't taken time to listen to God! When He spoke to me, I immediately put it into my own setting – what I was doing – where I was going. I didn't open my spirit more to fully listen to Him. Even when I arrived home and the impression came back, I didn't stop the hurried process involved in getting ready to leave on that trip and take time to listen. As A.L. and I talked later, we realized that God had spoken to both of us several times about what was going to happen, but we hadn't realized it. We hadn't stopped to listen.

Even in a life and death situation, God hadn't "knocked us over the head." The choice to listen was ours. Sometimes, God will keep coming back, but many times He does not.

A Book Holds a Snake and a Frog Explodes

One day I was dusting the books on our library shelves and suddenly the feeling came that I had just touched something that was very evil. I stopped dusting and thought, What could be evil here? Then I asked the Lord to show me what He was speaking about. As I prayed, I touched each book in that section. Suddenly, I knew I had come in contact with an evil spirit.

I took the book that we had been given and went into the living room to read it. As I sat down, God said, "If I say it's evil, why do you need to read it?" There was a fire burning in the fireplace. I crinkled some of the pages of the book and placed it on the fire. As the book rested on the logs in the fireplace a snake of fire began to come out from the main fire and move across the hearth. My mind refused to believe what I was seeing. At first there was just a protrusion of fire in one area and then it came out farther and farther until there was the shape of a snake about eight inches long curling out from the fire. It was about three inches in diameter.

I will never forget the battle I had with my mind. I couldn't believe what I was seeing. A.L. and the children were upstairs in the game room playing table-tennis and their laughter was ringing through the house. The noise of laughter was in heavy contrast with the evil in the room where I was. Then I spoke, "In the name of Jesus, snake, I command you to return to that fireplace. I command you, book, to burn in the name of Jesus!" Instantly the fire-snake went backwards into the fire, and the book began to burn.

Another time I was sitting at my desk when I had a feeling of evil present in a storage closet across the room. I walked over to the closet, opened the door and began to let my eyes travel over the contents. I stood praying in the spirit and just looked from shelf to shelf. Soon my eyes were drawn to a children's game. I picked up the box and realized it was a game of dragon warfare. Immediately, I destroyed the game. It took only a few minutes from the time I felt the evil until the Lord had shown me what it was and it was destroyed.

We hear of people looking for demons everywhere. We don't need to do that. Instead, we need to listen to the Holy Spirit when He speaks to our spirit. We will know when there is evil that we should do something about. Instead of looking for evil, we should concentrate on staying in the presence of God. Then the evil around us, if there is any, will become evident. Satan loves it when believers become so centered on looking for evil that they lose time that could be spent in the presence of the Lord.

Another incident occurred many years ago, as A.L. and I were having breakfast with some people in our weekend mountain home. Some months before, we had been given a ceramic frog that was about twelve inches high. We hadn't liked the frog, but hadn't wanted to offend the people who had given it to us, so we set it by the fireplace. That morning while we were talking about the Lord, my eyes would continually be drawn to that frog. Finally, I interrupted the flow of conversation. "A.L. there is something wrong with that frog. Let's get rid of it!"

A.L. walked over to pick up the frog. He said later he was thinking, I'll just throw it off the deck and smash it on the rocks below. But as his hands were about four inches from that thing, it exploded in all directions.

That frog had been sitting there for weeks. But that morning, as we were talking about the Lord, as the presence of the Lord filled the room, the evil thing in that frog became obvious. Then we moved to destroy it. Both A.L. and I had remarked about how much we disliked it soon after it was given to us, but we hadn't realized that the dislike was coming from our spirits not from our emotions.

I don't think demons prefer to be in objects. They would rather be in people. However, they will, if given an opportunity, come into an object so that they can remain in our homes undetected. There are certain objects they prefer such as frogs, owls and other creatures of the night. They also can be found in replicas of items used in idol worship and witchcraft. All of these items must be discerned, renounced and destroyed. Often we've "given place to the devil" allowing spirits of deception into our lives.

As we're sensitive to the Holy Spirit, He will reveal these items to us. When we're quick to obey God, regardless of the value or sentimental attachment to these objects, we will close the door through which demon spirits can attack and deceive us.

A Tornado in the House

The main purpose of distinguishing between spirits is our protection. It's for our physical protection, our spiritual protection, the protection of others, and the liberation of people from satanic bondage through deliverance. We receive the gift of distinguishing between spirits so that we will know what Satan has planned and how we can stop those plans. By operating in this gift of the Holy Spirit, evil can be kept out of the midst of the body of Christ.

About ten-thirty one night, I was working at my computer in our home, as usual, hurrying to finish some project. A.L. had come home from weeks of ministry in a foreign country and had gone to bed, exhausted. As I was typing, I kept having the impression to go into Cindy's room. Our daughter was sharing an apartment with another girl and wasn't living at home at this time. The impression became stronger. I stood up and started across the office toward her room. As I did, a tornado of evil raced from her room toward me. It was huge. It was powerful! I knew I didn't want to come against that thing by myself.

I knew that one can put a thousand to flight, but two can put ten thousand to flight (Deuteronomy 32:30). I knew I needed A.L. with me in this battle and I ran down the stairs screaming, "A.L., A.L., wake up! Wake Up!" I banged my hand against the door to our room still shouting even as I opened it.

A.L. was jolted out of his sleep, and even his jet lag, by my explosive entry! "What's wrong? What's wrong?" he shouted. Once I knew he was thoroughly awake, my voice was more normal. I told him about the tornado which neither of us could see by then. Through a word of knowledge, we understood Cindy's life was being threatened. We prayed. We bound Satan. The battle went on, and we didn't let up for two and a half hours. We prayed in the Spirit. We prayed in English. We were battling for our daughter's life and we knew it. We didn't know where Cindy was. She had no telephone. There was nothing in the natural that we could do to help her. Finally, about one o'clock our spirits were suddenly at peace. We knew she was all right and we both went to bed.

Cindy called early the next morning. Instantly I asked, "What happened about ten-thirty last night?"

"How do you know something happened?" she replied. I told her about the danger we had felt and how we had continued in battle until about one that morning.

She had been driving home from work, when a former boyfriend had stopped her along the road side. He had been drinking and was becoming violent. He was talking murder and suicide.

He had grabbed the keys out of her Volkswagen Baja and wrenched the distributor cap off the engine. But Cindy had stayed calm talking to him for hours. She searched for the extra key hidden in the bottom of her purse. When she found it, she kept it hidden in her hand, and still talking calmly, she had taken the distributor cap and pushed it back into place. Of course, she had no way of knowing if she had put it back on properly. She climbed into the car and slid the extra key into the ignition. He started laughing at her, he knew the car wouldn't start with the distributor cap just pushed on in any position – but it did!

Cindy sped away from him, went to her apartment by a round-about route and hid her car in the back.

How did I know Cindy was in danger? What was the evil tornado I mentioned? As I had walked toward Cindy's room, the evil cloud that was in her room narrowed itself down to come through the door. The "head" that was approaching me was small with all that evil behind it and it looked just like the pictures I've seen of tornadoes, except it was moving horizontally through the house. The Holy Spirit had nudged me to go to her room so that He could expose the danger that was hiding there. I didn't "see" it until I moved in obedience and started in that direction.

It's difficult to describe how you see in the spirit realm. I see everything in its normal state – the furniture, the walls, the windows, the doors, but I also see the spirit being. It's as though it's transparent and I see it and see through it at the same time. When I turned and ran down the stairs, I had the impression of it being right behind me, but I didn't see it again.

A Second Battle

Several years later, I was walking through our house turning off the lights, when suddenly the form of a large "man" was about a foot in front of me. Of course, I nearly jumped out of my skin. Then I realized it was an evil spirit. When I called A.L. it disappeared, but it didn't go away. We began to pray.

A.L. knew in his spirit that this was a "confrontation" that involved our son. We bound Satan and in a short time we were at peace and went to bed. This time, however, we never found out what had happened.

Usually when we come into these situations, I am the one who has the first knowledge of evil. As we pray, A.L. or I both move in the word of knowledge. Then, it's usually A.L. who receives the word of wisdom to know what to do with the knowledge we've received. It's very important to move in all three of the revelation gifts of the Holy Spirit. The distinguishing between spirits could be a frightening thing without the operation of the word of knowledge and the word of wisdom.

The distinguishing between spirits is for our protection and for the protection of our loved ones, our friends, or others in the body of Christ.

Distinguishing between spirits can operate in many different ways. Our God is a God of variety. Sometimes it is a "knowing" in our spirits – a "seeing" in the spirit world – an "understanding" of a situation. Sometimes it's seeing a symbol. Sometimes it's a shaking in our spirit. The list of ways the Lord operates could never be complete. Once we allow the Holy Spirit to operate in this area of our lives, He will!

Chapter Five

Testing a Prophecy

A Prophecy Takes Root and Grows

If a prophecy is given to you and you don't distinguish between spirits, if you don't recognize a false prophecy and reject it, it will take root in your inner being. We must not be gullible. We must not sit like sponges and accept everything that comes to us as though it's from God. We must not absorb everything into our spirits.

If a prophecy isn't from God, it will produce seeds that are evil and these seeds will cause damage. Seeds always produce after their kind. Seeds from God produce blessings. Seeds from the human nature produce fruit of the soul. Seeds planted by the devil produce destruction and death.

We must never receive a prophecy without holding it up to the light of God's Word and to His Holy Spirit.

John wrote, Dear friends, do not believe every spirit, but test the spirits to see whether they are from God, because many false prophets have gone out into the world. This is how you can recognize the Spirit of God: Every spirit that acknowledges that Jesus Christ has come in the flesh is from God, but every spirit that does not acknowledge Jesus is not from God. This is the spirit of the antichrist, which you have heard is coming and even now is already in the world (1 John 4:1-3).

The spirit of antichrist is anything that is against Christ. Satan and every one of his demons are against Christ.

In the early seventies, there were many prophecies given that weren't from God. Almost everyone we knew received the same type of word. They were to receive a new car, change jobs, move across the country, handle large sums of money for the Lord, and have a great ministry. These prophecies of a great new future made them dissatisfied with the present. They thought the job they had wasn't the one God had chosen for them. The money they handled wasn't as much as God had for them in the future. Talking to a neighbor about Jesus wasn't as important as the great ministry God had called them to do. Many people who received these prophecies let seeds of discontent grow in their hearts.

Some believed the prophecies so much they tried to make them come true. They quit their jobs expecting a great new job. Some even packed their things waiting for the move across the country. They purchased cars they couldn't afford. They became gullible and were drawn into financial schemes which cost them thousands of dollars. These people were genuinely committed believers, but they had been deceived by Satan. Now, many of them are no longer committed to a local church. They are wounded in their spirits. They wonder how God could have let them down, why those things He promised didn't come to pass. God didn't let them down!

They hadn't been taught to distinguish between spirits and even today, as they try to go on with the business of living, they don't understand it was evil spirits, not God, that brought them to this place.

The first time A.L. was in Malaysia, he flew into a small airport on the east coast of that country. There he was met by John Ezekiel, a man he had never seen before. As they drove for miles back into the jungle, A.L. began to prophesy over John. He told him that God said he was to start a Bible school. He told him that God said he, John, was the evangelist that God was going to use to reach his country. None of what he was saying made sense in the natural realm to A.L.. John was an unknown minister, hidden in what A.L. refers to as the "uttermost part of the earth." And yet as A.L. spoke on and on, he knew the message was from God. John was visibly moved in his spirit. What A.L. was prophesying over him was confirmation of the things God had been speaking to John and his wife for several months. They turned the church over to another minister and moved across the country as God had directed. They started a Bible school. They started another church. Today, John is traveling all over the world as an evangelist. Many doors are open to him and he is making a mighty impact for the Lord in his own nation.

When A.L. gave John this prophecy, it came as a confirmation of the things God had already spoken. God spoke to John through the gift of prophecy to encourage him.

Every prophecy must be tested. It may be from a human spirit. It may be from an evil spirit. It may be from God.

How to Test a Prophecy

There are seven tests we should give a prophecy. They can be of great benefit in keeping your life free from deception.

➡ Does the Prophecy Agree with Scripture?

A prophecy that is from the Spirit of God can never contradict the written Word of God. God doesn't change and He doesn't change His written Word. There are no "special exceptions."

Paul warned us, **But even if we or an angel from heaven should preach a gospel other than the one we preached to you, let him be eternally condemned! (Galatians 1:8).**

In Malachi 3:6 we read, **'I the Lord do not change...'**

The writer of the book of Hebrews wrote, **Jesus Christ is the same yesterday and today and forever (Hebrews 13:8).**

➡ Know the Fruit

It's true that only God can judge a person, but every one of us is responsible to know the fruits of those who are having an influence on our lives.

Matthew wrote, Watch out for false prophets. They come to you in sheep's clothing, but inwardly they are ferocious wolves. By their fruit you will recognize them. Do people pick grapes from thornbushes, or figs from thistles? Likewise every good tree bears good fruit, but a bad tree bears bad fruit. A good tree cannot bear bad fruit, and a bad tree cannot bear good fruit. Every tree that does not bear good fruit is cut down and thrown into the fire. Thus, by their fruit you will recognize them (Matthew 7:15-20).

Paul gives a good description of both good fruit and bad fruit. The acts of the sinful nature are obvious: sexual immorality, impurity and debauchery; idolatry and witchcraft; hatred, discord, jealousy, fits of rage, selfish ambition, dissensions, factions and envy; drunkenness, orgies, and the like. I warn you, as I did before, that those who live like this will not inherit the kingdom of God.

But the fruit of the Spirit is love, joy, peace, patience, kindness, goodness, faithfulness, gentleness and self-control. Against such things there is no law (Galatians 5:19-23).

➡ Does the Prophecy Glorify Christ?

Does the message glorify Christ or does it glorify the person giving the message? Does the message bring glory to the person receiving the message?

But when he, the Spirit of truth, comes, he will guide you into all truth. He will not speak on his own; he will speak only what he hears, and he will tell you what is yet to come. He will bring glory to me by taking from what is mine and making it known to you (John 16:13,14).

At this I fell at his feet to worship him. But he said to me, 'Do not do it! I am a fellow servant with you and with your brothers who hold to the testimony of Jesus. Worship God! For the testimony of Jesus is the spirit of prophecy' (Revelation 19:10).

Many times if you listen to a prophecy with your spirit, words will jump out at you. Words like, "Listen to my prophet, he is a man chosen by me to fulfill a special ministry." "This is my prophet, he has ministered faithfully for me for many years." Listen for words that lift up the person giving the prophecy. They aren't from God.

A false message may instill pride in the person receiving the prophecy. "I've chosen you above all others..." Or, "You are the person chosen by me for a special ministry that no other could fulfill..." Prophecies of this kind aren't from God.

➨ **Is the Prophecy Fulfilled?**

If the message is from God, it will come to pass. Perhaps not in the time frame of our choice, but it will happen. When a person hears a message from God, a common tendency is for us to try to make it happen in the natural realm. This will bring disappointment and heartache.

You may say to yourselves, 'How can we know when a message has not been spoken by the Lord?' If what a prophet proclaims in the name of the Lord does not take place or come true, that is a message the Lord has not spoken. That prophet has spoken presumptuously. Do not be afraid of him (Deuteronomy 18:21-22).

'But I the Lord will speak what I will, and it shall be fulfilled without delay. For in your days, you rebellious house, I will fulfill whatever I say', declares the Sovereign Lord (Ezekiel 12:25).

➡ Does the Prophecy Lead Toward God?

A prophecy from the Lord will always lead us closer to Him. A false message will lead us away from God.

If a prophet, or one who foretells by dreams, appears among you and announces to you a miraculous sign or wonder, and if the sign or wonder of which he has spoken takes place, and he says, 'Let us follow other gods' (gods you have not known) 'and let us worship them,' you must not listen to the words of that prophet or dreamer. The Lord your God is testing you to find out whether you love him with all your heart and with all your soul (Deuteronomy 13:1-3a).

➡ Does Prophecy Bring Liberty or Bondage?

If a message causes a person who is seeking to serve God to feel depressed, grieved, or heavy in his or her spirit, it's not from God. Sometimes God will bring correction, but that will only be through a spiritual leader. It will be delivered, usually not in a public meeting, without condemnation and it will bring a sense of relief to the person receiving it. Relief will come because that person would have felt something was amiss, but didn't understand what it was.

But everyone who prophesies speaks to men for their strengthening, encouragement and comfort (1 Corinthians 14:3).

For you did not receive a spirit that makes you a slave again to fear, but you received the Spirit of sonship. And by him we cry, 'Abba, Father' (Romans 8:15).

➼ What Is the Inner Witness of the Spirit?

We have the Holy Spirit within us and as we learn to operate in the gift of distinguishing between spirits, He will witness to us if the message is from God.

I keep asking that the God of our Lord Jesus Christ, the glorious Father, may give you the Spirit of wisdom and revelation, so that you may know him better. I pray also that the eyes of your heart may be enlightened in order that you may know the hope to which he has called you, the riches of his glorious inheritance in the saints, and his incomparably great power for us who believe. That power is like the working of his mighty strength (Ephesians 1:17-19).

Prophecy is a gift of the Holy Spirit. We mustn't refuse to operate in this gift because of the times it has been misused. Instead, we must learn to judge it carefully to be certain it is from God. Then we should walk in faith and boldness and let God work out that prophecy in our lives.

Chapter Six

Con-Artists in the Church

False Leaders in My Nice Church?

Paul warned the early Christians that there were false apostles. Paul said there were not only false apostles, but that Satan disguises himself as an angel of light, and there were also false ministers.

For such men are false apostles, deceitful workmen, masquerading as apostles of Christ. And no wonder, for Satan himself masquerades as an angel of light. It is not surprising, then, if his servants masquerade as servants of righteousness. Their end will be what their actions deserve (2 Corinthians 11:13-15).

Paul had more to say on the subject when he wrote to Timothy, The Spirit clearly says that in later times some will abandon the faith and follow deceiving spirits and things taught by demons. Such teachings come through hypocritical liars, whose consciences have been seared as with a hot iron (1 Timothy 4:1,2).

But mark this: There will be terrible times in the last days. People will be lovers of themselves, lovers of money, boastful, proud, abusive, disobedient to their parents, ungrateful, unholy, without love, unforgiving, slanderous, without self-control, brutal, not lovers of the good, treacherous, rash, conceited, lovers of pleasure rather than lovers of God—having a form of godliness but denying its power. Have nothing to do with them.

They are the kind who worm their way into homes and gain control over weak-willed women, who are loaded down with sins and are swayed by all kinds of evil desires, always learning but never able to acknowledge the truth. Just as Jannes and Jambres opposed Moses, so also these men oppose the truth—men of depraved minds, who, as far as the faith is concerned, are rejected.

But they will not get very far because, as in the case of those men, their folly will be clear to everyone (2 Timothy 3:1-90).

How is their folly to be made clear to everyone? Often this revelation will come to believers through the gift of distinguishing between spirits.

The First Step May Be Repentance

Remember how I had closed the door to the gift of distinguishing between spirits? Of course, I had asked the Lord's forgiveness within a short time. However, for a number of years, I still didn't operate in the clear gift of distinguishing between spirits that we need for the days in which we now live. What I had done was wrong. I prayed, "God, forgive me for closing the door. Give me back the operation of the spiritual gift of the distinguishing between spirits the way it was before we were involved in so much confusion in our spirits. Make it the way it was before I shut the door. God, I realize we can't survive without it. Now, by faith, once again, I receive and release this gift to operate in my life."

Perhaps, as you have been reading this book, you have realized that when the spiritual gift of distinguishing between spirits began to operate in your life, you haven't received it. Perhaps, like A.L. and me, you thought you had a critical spirit and put those thoughts aside. You may even have decided, just as I did, you didn't want to operate in this gift. To quench the manifestations of the Holy Spirit, even in ignorance, is sin.

If this is your situation, it's time to get rid of the sin. All we need to do according to 1 John 1:9 is to confess that sin. **If we confess our sins, he is faithful and just and will forgive us our sins and purify us from all unrighteousness.**

The next step is to do just as Paul instructed Timothy – to stir up the gift we have already received. Paul wrote, **For this reason I remind you to fan into flame the gift of God, which is in you through the laying on of my hands (2 Timothy 1:6).** That is what I began to do.

About a week after I prayed about stirring up the gift of distinguishing between spirits, I was visiting a church. A man stood up to minister. He was an associate pastor in another church and a personal friend of the pastor of the church I was visiting. As he started to minister to the people, I knew the man was covered with lust demons. I closed my eyes. That doesn't help when you are seeing in the spirit, however! I prayed, "Okay, God, now I know I am operating again in distinguishing between spirits and now I can forget all about this, right?" Obviously, I was wrong!

Do Something!

What is the purpose of revelation? It's given so that we can do something about the situation! And yet, I had no release from the Father to cast those demons out. I wasn't in a position of leadership in the meeting. Nevertheless, I could and did bind those demonic spirits during the service.

Well, that's the end of that! I thought as I was leaving the meeting. I thanked the Lord for bringing back the gift of distinguishing between spirits and planned to go on my way. Wrong, again!

For three weeks, God wouldn't let me forget what He had shown me. Finally, I was listening to a tape by another Christian brother on responsibility to the body of Christ, and I said out loud, "God, if You make an opening, I will talk to the pastor about it." That was quite safe. At that time, I think the pastor and I only talked two or three times a year on a personal level.

He called me within an hour! As we were discussing this and that, in my spirit I knew what God was doing. I couldn't enjoy the conversation. Even as we talked, I was praying and arguing with God. I prayed, "God, You know they're personal friends... See, we're not even on the subject."

The conversation stopped. The pastor said, "Joyce, do you operate in the discerning of spirits?" God made the opening, and then I shared with the pastor what I knew in the spirit.

Sitting in the Pew

Since most of us aren't the pastors or elders of the church, it's important that we understand how we can operate in the distinguishing between spirits when we're participating in a service.

For example, you are enjoying a time of praise and worship in your church, and a person walks in the door and suddenly you know that person is being influenced by a demon. What do you do? God has revealed the demon to you for a reason. You are a participant in the service. While you may not be responsible as the leader of that service, you do share in the corporate responsibility with the other believers. Do you jump up and shout, "That person is full of demons!"? No! You would probably be the one cast out. You can bind those demons and limit their ability to manifest during that meeting.

We don't have authority to cast demons out of a person who may want them, or from one who has made openings for them to come in, without the cooperation of that person. However, we can bind them from operating during a meeting and we can stop them from hindering that person from receiving the message God has for them.

Our authority is over demons and not over other humans. We must operate in spiritual authority within the boundaries of responsibility that God has given us.

Jesus said, 'I have given you authority to trample on snakes and scorpions and to overcome all the power of the enemy; nothing will harm you' (Luke 10:19).

Jesus also said, 'I tell you the truth, the Son can do nothing by himself; he can do only what he sees his Father doing, because whatever the Father does the Son also does' (John 5:19).

Jesus cast out demons everywhere He went, however we know He didn't cast out every demon He came in contact with. If He had, He wouldn't have been crucified.

What if the church is having a guest speaker and the pastor or leading elder looks over and suddenly receives the revelation that demons are in operation within that person? The person responsible for that meeting does have the responsibility to stop that person from ministering. That is the reason most ministers will not allow someone to minister in their church until they know them, or they are recommended by someone they know and respect.

The public expression of the vocal gifts, or revelation gifts, of the Holy Spirit must be subject to the authority of the spiritual leadership of that meeting. However, any believer in a group can pray and bind Satan and the manifestation of evil spirits which have been revealed. That is where we win the battle.

Standing Behind the Pulpit

The saddest thing to realize as we discuss the con-artist in the church is that there are also many who are accepted as "ministers" either of local churches, traveling ministries, or radio and television ministries, who are very experienced con-artists.

A friend of ours who travels from city to city setting up large meetings for several ministries, was in Africa in 1989. He had gone to Africa to set up a large crusade for a well-known American ministry. We met him as he first returned to the United States and he looked very distraught. "What's wrong?" A.L. asked as soon as he saw him.

Our friend began to pour out his distress over what he had seen in that country. He had been met at the airport by a person in a large Rolls Royce. They had driven to the palatial home of the man who was to be the contact man in that country and there were several more very expensive cars in his driveway.

As our friend began the work of setting up the meetings, he was asked, "How much are you going to bless the pastors with so that they will bring their people to the meetings?"

"Bless the pastors?" our friend replied.

"Yes, how much are you going to give them to bring their people?"

"You mean, we're to pay the pastors to bring their people?"

"Yes," the man replied. "That is the way we operate in this nation. That is the way that we assemble the large crowds for the crusades here."

Our friend replied, "That's a bribe! That's not of God!" Of course, the contact man, sitting in his large prestigious home, expected to receive a large percentage as well. When our friend returned to the States, he made inquiries and found this to be true. Ministries are paying pastors to bring their people so they can hold huge crusades.

In Romans 16:18, we read, **For such people are not serving our Lord Christ, but their own appetites. By smooth talk and flattery they deceive the minds of naive people.** Notice that it's by smooth talk and flattery that they deceive. Our minds can be deceived by the enticing words of men. That is the reason we must learn to operate in the distinguishing between spirits.

While our friend was in that part of the world, he spent time and money traveling to several other mission projects that he knew about personally. He knew that thousands, even millions of dollars had been collected in the United States for these projects, but as he visited one after another, he found nothing had been done. The most he found in place after place was an old sign on a piece of land that said, "Future Home of _____," but very little, or none, of the money had gone for the project.

Well-meaning people had sacrificially given to these projects thinking their money was being used as the Lord directed. Instead, it had been going into the pockets of unscrupulous manipulators. These false projects have drained financing from many God-ordained ministries.

The answer isn't to stop giving! The answer is to know the spirits of those to whom we give. The answer is to investigate in the spirit, but also in the natural realm.

On the other side, A.L. and I've been privileged to meet many sincere men and women of God who have made much personal sacrifice to do the work of Jesus. These people haven't resorted to the commercial fund raising methods that are so prominent in our land. Instead, they are simply sharing their God-given visions and telling what God is doing through their ministries. They are sowing seeds and believing God to bring in the needed finances.

Jesus warned in Matthew 24:4, '**Watch out that no one deceives you.**' Jesus was speaking about false Christs coming. But notice, He said, "Watch out." We are to watch out. It's up to us.

Paul warned us in Acts 20:28 and 29, **Keep watch over yourselves and all the flock of which the Holy Spirit has made you overseers. Be shepherds of the church of God, which he bought with his own blood. I know that after I leave, savage wolves will come in among you and will not spare the flock.**

So often, we've used these verses as a warning only against false doctrine or false prophecies. Today, the wolves have entered our churches and they are using them as places to practice their lucrative con-games of deception. In many cases, those presenting the "get rich quick" schemes have themselves been deceived by others and don't know the truth themselves.

These "wolves" are preying upon unsuspecting believers who would do well to listen to their spirits and operate in the spiritual gift of the distinguishing between spirits. They would do well to trust the inner witness of their spirits even though it seems that "everyone else is getting involved."

Chapter Seven

Gullible Christians

Gullible Christian Investors

During the years that A.L. and I were involved with the gold mining operation, we began to refer to ourselves and others like us as GCIs, "Gullible Christian Investors." Over the years, an understanding of what happened has come to us.

We knew that God had promised to supply all our needs according to His riches in glory. We knew we were to go into nation after nation teaching believers and preaching the Gospel of Jesus Christ. We knew we would be establishing Bible schools around the world. This would take money – a large amount of money. We knew God would provide the money to do the things He had given us to do. Therefore, when we were told that because we were a small ministry with a vision of reaching the world and others wanted to help us reach that goal, we believed they were sent by God to do exactly that.

The lady who first approached A.L. was the mother of one of his Bible School students. Most of the contacts to sell this bogus stock, that we know about, were made in churches or Bible study settings. Most of the people talking about the "opportunity" to invest in the "Christian" company were committed Christians who had been deceived and knew nothing about the "dark side" of the operation.

Multilevel Marketing

Some people have wrongfully used the church as a source of contacts to solicit people to become distributors in their multilevel business "opportunity." One time a lady called and invited us to dinner since both of our daughters were rooming together at a Christian university. After a hard day at work, we drove for two hours to get to their home only to discover the invitation to dinner was really given to get us to a multilevel presentation. That is deception and it's going on over and over again in Christian circles. It's not wrong to be involved in multilevel businesses, but it is wrong to practice deception in any area of our lives.

At a different time, A.L. and I decided that since multilevel sales were the only area of sales in which we had not been involved, we would become involved with three companies and learn how they operated. We were interested in learning if multilevel marketing was suited for Christian literature. What we found was interesting. In at least two of the organizations, there were strong controlling spirits and spirits of deception in operation. Sitting through their sales presentations was like sitting in Satan's kingdom. Needless to say, we couldn't stay involved in those organizations.

We were recently told about a sales meeting in a multilevel organization in the United States in which the people stood and raised their hands as the leader held up a large piece of jade. The tears were streaming down their faces as they gave homage to, or were actually worshiping, the company represented by that piece of jade. They were declaring their gratitude to this company for the financial opportunity that it had provided them. That is not business, that is idolatry!

People are often told that they shouldn't waste their time with people who aren't going to become productive members of their "down-line" organization. Is that Christian? Nowhere in scripture are we instructed to look to every person for what that person can do for us. Instead, we're instructed to reach out in love to those in need – to those who aren't in any position to be of help to us.

Often multilevel companies encourage or give incentives for people to drive luxury cars and to wear expensive furs and jewelry. This is to lure others into signing up to be distributors. One writer aptly referred to this as, "Fake It Till You Make It." I don't want to imply that all multilevel marketing programs are bad. There is, however, a need to operate in the spiritual gift of distinguishing between spirits in this area. We must obey the words of Jesus when He said, 'Watch out that no one deceives you' (Matthew 24:4).

Whenever the pursuit of money becomes our goal, we're headed for deception. When the pursuit of money, or of things, becomes our goal, we move into bondage. We must spend more and more time to achieve the goal and we have less and less time to spend doing the works of Jesus. Our walk with the Lord is usually the first thing to suffer and then the time that we have for our family, our friends and our church.

Other Con-Games

In Texas, one of the most common investment "opportunities" to reach into the Christian area is the promotion of new oil wells. Drilling for oil is a very risky venture. Christians are often led to believe that because the Lord said this or that, this particular venture is different.

The difference between a legitimate business proposition that goes bad and a scam operation is the use of the money that is invested. If the money goes into the business and it simply doesn't produce a profit, it was just a bad business deal. If the investors' money is taken out for high living expenses or other personal investments by the directors or other controlling people, and there never was any intention of making a profit with the investors' money, it was a con-operation.

Some Christians can afford to invest a small percentage of their savings in "risky venture" opportunities with the possibility of large profits. However, all too often, these well-meaning Christians have been deceived into investing most, or all, of their savings in risky projects which they are told are "certain" because of God's blessing.

They aren't financially prepared to suffer such highly probable losses.

Individual Con-Artists

There are hundreds of individual con-artists operating in churches. In Houston, there was a man who approached several of the women in the church separately, with a morally improper proposal. Women would come to us and tell us how the night before they could hardly make this man leave them alone and then they would see him standing in the aisle on Sunday morning with his hands raised as though in praise to God. "God knows we need sex," this man would say, "It's a normal part of the body He has given us. Sex is not wrong!" Then, as they would answer with the scripture, he would reply, "Well, even if it might be sin, all we need to do in the morning is ask God to forgive us."

It's not always the man approaching the woman either. Sometimes, it's the woman approaching the man.

God's Word is true. The words of Exodus 20:14, **You shall not commit adultery,** cannot be rationalized away. We live in a society where thousands live in the deception that this is no longer a sin.

When we were on staff at a large church in Southern California, we became acquainted with a lady who attended every service. She was always there and she usually sat in one of the front row seats. She wanted to be seen. She would raise her hands and seem to enter into worship.

After the service, she would approach someone with her story. According to her, she was a missionary sent out by that church, but she had been instructed to raise her own support. She would tell exciting stories of ministry and the person she approached would often give her twenty-five, fifty, even a hundred dollars. The problem was, she wasn't a missionary from that church or any other, and there was no ministry! After a time, the staff became aware of what she was doing and, if they saw her, would approach the groups and tell them the truth. She became very adept at staying out of their sight and would talk to people in the parking lot or on the sidewalk.

We were in another church in Texas and the same type of thing would happen. There, an alcoholic man would approach someone after church with the story about how he had just gotten right with God and had this job offer in a nearby city, but his car had broken down. He was a pretty good judge of people and from one he would gain fifteen dollars, from another fifty. He used the money to buy alcohol and would be back as soon as the money ran out.

There was nothing the church staff could do except keep it from happening in the church and on the church property when they were aware that it was happening. The last time I saw the lady "missionary," she was more expensively dressed than most of the congregation. She was still acquiring money from well-meaning, misled Christians. It would be wonderful if these situations were isolated incidents, but they are not!

Our Solution

The only solution is for every believer to listen to the Spirit of God and to know the spirit of those who approach them. These are examples of the small con-artists, but there are international con-artists who are working church people for money. It would be hard to count the thousands, and even millions, of dollars that have been taken from unsuspecting Christians through much more elaborate schemes.

Peter warned us in 2 Peter 1:1-4, **Grace and peace be yours in abundance through the knowledge of God and of Jesus our Lord. His divine power has given us everything we need for life and godliness through our knowledge of him who called us by his own glory and goodness. Through these he has given us his very great and precious promises, so that through them you may participate in the divine nature and escape the corruption in the world caused by evil desires. It is through the Word of God, through the promises of God that we are kept from the corruption of this world.**

A business person once said to A.L. and me, "Christians are the most gullible of all people." That is because we move in love, and think that everyone else is doing the same. We are honest and so we tend to believe that others are honest. We have integrity and we believe others do, also. It's time we learned to protect ourselves by walking in the Spirit. It's time every believer learned to test every spirit.

Chapter Eight

Are We Defenseless?

Against Demon Spirits

Are we unprotected against demon spirits?

No, absolutely not! Jesus has defeated every single demon on the face of the earth, or under the earth, or in the heavens, or wherever they might be! Every single demon knows it has been defeated by Jesus Christ. The demons know it. God knows it. The problem is that Christians don't seem to know it.

The demons have been defeated, but we, the believers, still let them spread their deceit. These "masters of deception" have been going undetected in the churches and in the lives of believers. The truth is, we've been trying to discern situations with our own minds. Yet, God has given us a supernatural perception and protection through the spiritual gift of distinguishing between spirits. We must receive God's revelation of these spirits of deception and command them to leave in the name of Jesus. When demons hear someone speak who knows his or her authority in Jesus, they obey.

Demons try to intimidate and frighten Christians by making them believe that they are big and strong. They try to keep Christians from discovering their overcoming authority in Jesus Christ. Demons are committed to schemes of deception that will bring defeat into the lives of Christians. However, God has provided a supernatural means of victory over deception for every believer.

We, as believers in Jesus, have authority over all the power of the enemy. We can walk confidently in our God-given authority. We have God's power, the power of the Holy Spirit within us! When we realize this, we can win the world to Jesus in a short time! When Christians understand the gifts of the Holy Spirit, when they know who they are in Jesus, when they operate in total obedience to the Holy Spirit, they will no longer live in defeat.

The Test of a Spirit

How do we test the spirits around us? They may be in another person, in an object, in a radio or television program, in the music or in the area surrounding us. The evil spirits are in the spirit realm and that is all around us. The good news is that angels are also in the spirit realm and they are also all around us! And there are two angels to every demon!

God didn't intend that we should be defenseless against evil spirits. He has commanded us to test the spirits, and He has given us instructions on how this is to be done.

This is how you can recognize the Spirit of God: Every spirit that acknowledges that Jesus Christ has come in the flesh is from God, but every spirit that does not acknowledge Jesus is not from God (1 John 4:2,3).

One time when A.L. and I were involved in a personal deliverance, the demons began to speak through the voice of the person to whom we were ministering. We heard demons shout, "Jesus is Lord. Jesus is Lord." I can tell you from personal experience that demons can say "Jesus is Lord." They spoke these words in a sing-song way, and the sound was very antagonistic. Now, we have learned to bind the demons. We don't want to hear anything from them! They are of their father and he is the Father of Lies.

A demon can say "Jesus." A demon can say "Jesus is Lord." What, then, is the test of a spirit? John tells us that the demons cannot acknowledge that Jesus Christ has come in the flesh and is from God.

Years ago, before we knew the reality of the demon world, we were visiting a friend's home and they were playing games. One of the games was a Ouija board. We didn't think anything was wrong about it. We sat down and began playing with that board, too. It was answering questions quite accurately. As the evening progressed, I had become tired of the "game" and was talking to some friends sitting to my right. My left hand was still on the pointer and A.L. was asking it some questions. My hand was moving along with A.L.'s on the pointer all over that board.

I was ignoring the board and A.L.'s questions to it, talking to friends, when all of a sudden my left hand flew across the board and up into the air over my head. My whole arm was twisted violently and I felt a tremendous anger come against me.

In shock, I looked at A.L. and said, "What did you ask?"

A.L. had asked the Ouija board, "What do you say to the shed blood of Jesus Christ?"

When he had asked that question, my hand had slapped the pointer across the board to the word "good-by" and then had flown up into the air.

This is the test of a spirit: "What do you say to the shed blood of Jesus Christ?"

(Yes, the time did come when we renounced all involvement with the Ouija board and asked God's forgiveness for being involved with it.)

If you receive a prophecy, if you receive a vision, if you receive any "word from the Lord," test it.

The Deceived Deceive Others

We met with a man many years ago whom we felt was in deception and was leading others into deception. Some mutual friends had asked us to meet with the man who they were considering taking into their ministry. They asked us to operate especially in distinguishing between spirits in this meeting. We spent several hours with the man and his wife and as we left them, we were puzzled for a time. We knew the man wasn't trying to deceive us. But we still knew in the spirit the fruit was wrong. It wasn't from God. Then God let us understand. The man wasn't trying to deceive us, he was deceived. He felt what he was doing was of God. Satan had deceived him, so we couldn't feel in our spirits any area in which he was consciously trying to deceive us.

We were concerned about his visions of angels and asked him during that meeting, "Did you test the angels? Did you ask them what they said to the shed blood of Jesus Christ?" His answer was that we didn't understand, the angels were too awesome for a mere human to test them.

What did Paul say? **But even if we or an angel from heaven should preach a gospel other than the one we preached to you, let him be eternally condemned! (Galatians 1:8).**

We are warned to test even the angels bringing messages.

Two Areas of Deception

There are two areas of deception – human and satanic. Men deceive others for many reasons, but financial gain and a desire for position and adoration are two of the main causes.

It's well-known that many donations come into a ministry during the last month of the year. It's the time of year when many believers look at their yearly finances and realize they want to give more to the Lord in that calendar year. Ministries know this. The Christmas season is also a season of tenderness in the human spirit.

Let me share with you one deception we know about from a ministry newsletter. We weren't involved in this ministry, but we knew people who were. The ministry hadn't made the payments on their facility for three months. They had the money, they just didn't make the payments. Then they sent out a newsletter saying, "We are three months behind on the payments on our facilities." This was true. They were behind. "If we don't pay this month they will take everything away from us." This statement also was true. The next sentence went something like, "If you don't make a sacrificial donation today, we will no longer have a ministry!" They received thousands and thousands of dollars.

The letter went out geared to the time when people would be the most sensitive, and people gave. The people who were praying about where God wanted them to put their money didn't give to this "crisis." They weren't manipulated. They weren't deceived.

In another situation, the pastor of a large church took all the money from the normal working church bank account and transferred it to another account. The following Sunday, he stood before the congregation and told them very "sincerely," very "honestly," that the church's bank account was a big fat zero. He held up his hand and made a big zero with his fingers. Then he said something like, "I know you people. I know when there is a need, you give and you give. I know you will give every cent you can to meet our need at this time." That is deception.

We've no idea what the size of the offering was that morning.

One time A.L. and I attended meetings in a small church in Southern California. As the pastor was preparing to take the offering, we asked the Lord how much we could give. We were expecting God to tell us a large amount. In another church that week, God had told us to give a thousand dollars. This time when we asked the Lord how much to give, He replied, "Not one penny!" to one of us, and, "Nothing" to the other. We were surprised, but we didn't put anything in the offering. A few months later, we learned that this man was taking most of the offerings for himself. The church wasn't even able to pay its bills. God hadn't wanted His money going to that man.

We are responsible to test the spirits. Usually when we do, we find the minister or ministry to be upright before God! Sometimes, they are not.

God says if we plant our seed in good soil, it will bring forth fruit. What happens when a person is deceived and plants his seed in soil that is choked by weeds? He feels, "God's Word isn't true. I planted seed, but I didn't reap a harvest." Sometimes, that is because the seed was planted in stony ground.

These are examples of human deception. There is also satanic deception.

John warns us, **Many deceivers, who do not acknowledge Jesus Christ as coming in the flesh, have** gone out into the world. Any such person is the deceiver and the antichrist (2 John 1:7).

Matthew wrote, For false Christs and false prophets will appear and perform great signs and miracles to deceive even the elect–if that were possible (Matthew 24:24).

We are responsible. When you are sitting in a service, listen with your spirit. You may feel your spirit almost leaping for joy and expanding. You'll feel a buoyancy, a closeness to God. Distinguishing between spirits is easy when that which is happening is of God.

Sometimes, you will feel your spirit feeling smaller and smaller. You may find yourself sitting almost slumped over and you are thinking about how bad you have been. Feelings of guilt and condemnation begin to rise up within your thoughts. Don't accept things that aren't from God. Learn to listen to that inner witness. We are instructed to judge every word we hear or read. Not only do we have the right, we have the responsibility, to judge it before God.

In two of Peter's statements, we're given examples of Jesus operating in the gift of distinguishing between spirits. The first statement followed Jesus asking the disciples whom they said He was. Simon Peter answered, 'You are the Christ, the Son of the living God.'

Jesus replied, 'Blessed are you, Simon son of Jonah, for this was not revealed to you by man, but by my Father in heaven (Matthew 16:16,17).

The second statement of Peter was from a different source. Jesus had told the disciples the things He was going to suffer, and Peter disagreed. Peter took him aside and began to rebuke him. 'Never, Lord!' he said. 'This shall never happen to you!'

Jesus turned and said to Peter, 'Get behind me, Satan! You are a stumbling block to me; you do not have in mind the things of God, but the things of men' (Matthew 16:22,23).

Peter was very close to Jesus. His intentions were good, but he was speaking from the wrong spirit.

A Good Saying from an Evil Source

The scripture concerning Paul and the fortune-telling girl puzzled me for years.

Once when we were going to the place of prayer, we were met by a slave girl who had a spirit by which she predicted the future. She earned a great deal of money for her owners by fortune-telling. This girl followed Paul and the rest of us, shouting, 'These men are servants of the Most High God, who are telling you the way to be saved.' She kept this up for many days. Finally Paul became so troubled that he turned around and said to the spirit, 'In the name of Jesus Christ I command you to come out of her!' At that moment the spirit left her (Acts 16:16-18).

Listen to what the damsel said, 'These men are servants of the Most High God who are telling you the way to be saved.'

It might be fun to walk through the airport and have someone start shouting, "These persons are from God telling you how to be saved!" It would be an open door! Just think how you could preach. What if you were in a shopping center and someone started shouting this and a crowd started gathering? That could be a wonderful opportunity to reach the lost!

I thought about this. This damsel was like a herald announcing who they were. What was wrong with that? What she said was true.

Then I started thinking that maybe she was shouting it while they were trying to teach and it was an interruption, but the scripture doesn't say that.

Notice that it says, **She kept this up for many days. Finally Paul became so troubled...** When she started, Paul was troubled. It went on the next day and it continued to trouble him, and then it went on the next day. The Bible says she continued many days. Finally, Paul became so troubled that he turned around and said to the spirit, '**In the name of Jesus Christ I command you to come out of her!**' It took Paul many days to decide to command that spirit to come out.

I mulled over this scripture for some time. "God, I still don't have an understanding. What she said was true, but it was from an evil spirit. We know a tree brings forth good or brings forth evil. Why did it take Paul many days? Since what she said was right, why did he stop her?" God opened a whole area of understanding for me.

Why would an evil spirit announce what was true? Why would an evil spirit want to promote Paul's ministry? What was the motive?

What the demon spirit within the girl desired was to travel with the apostles. The damsel and the evil spirit were doing this to gain credibility. They wanted to be seen and known as one traveling with the apostles. If Paul had allowed it to go on, when he and Silas had left town, she could have said, "I traveled with the apostles..." That would have given her implied authority.

This same thing is happening today. Evil spirits draw certain people to ministries, to pastors and to church leaders to gain acceptance. Later, they will say, "When I was traveling with Brother So-and-so, he said..." If the spirits of these people aren't recognized at once, they can do much damage to believers and to the ministry. They become a drain on the ministry both in the time they take and in the spirit realm. Yet, there are also people God will draw to the ministries, ministers and church leaders who are of God and their ministry is real.

How do you know a person's true motive? How do you know whether you should receive from a person or not? The answer is that every believer must operate in the spiritual gift of distinguishing between spirits. We cannot rely only on what another person says. We must know and trust this inner witness of His Spirit for ourselves.

Chapter Nine

This Gift Is for Today

A Former Witch Speaks Out

Several years ago, I spent about five hours with a lady who had been a witch and one of the head priestesses of the satanic church near Houston, Texas. She had participated in human sacrifices. However, even as she had reached that position in Satan's kingdom, there was a hunger in her heart to find God. She had accepted Jesus as her personal Savior a short time before we met. The hours I spent with her were a revelation to me. I hadn't realized the extent of the attack of witchcraft that was coming against our churches.

In her satanic church, there was a class instructing witches on Christian doctrine so they could talk "our language." The next step was to learn to blaspheme Christ in a foreign language. (In her case, she had learned Japanese swear words.) The witches memorized many phrases. Once they knew our doctrine and our "language," they would go into a local charismatic church and stand up and give a "message in tongues." This "message" was the blasphemy they had memorized. If the pastor or other leaders didn't speak against the "message," they would gain an easy entrance into that church.

Soon they would move into a place of "service." She told me they would then zero in on the leaders, the Sunday school teachers, those who were there on Wednesday night and people from the choir. They would invite these active church members into their homes for "Bible study" and in six short weeks, they could have many of them involved in Satan worship.

This is some of the attack that is coming against the body of Christ from the satanic church. Church leaders have an awesome responsibility to know those who labor among them.

Paul wrote, **And we beseech you, brethren, to know them which labor among you. (1 Thessalonians 5:12a).**

What if the pastor and other leaders do miss it? Most pastors tend to operate in compassion during a meeting. They might say, "Oh, I know that prophecy wasn't from God, but they're well meaning. It didn't hurt anyone."

I find I must disagree. Any time a person speaks a message as though it's from God, and it's not from God, people will be hurt. People who accept that message as being from God may take it as guidance, or it may bring condemnation, guilt, confusion, or deception into their lives. It allows mixture to become the normal experience.

When a False Message Comes

Let's take as an example a message that is given that isn't from God. It's not even from a human spirit that is saturated in the Word of God. The message is directly from Satan. What should we do?

The answer is different for people in different functions in that body. In a normal situation, the responsibility for knowing the spirit comes first to the person in leadership at that time. It may be the worship leader, a visiting minister, the pastor or other elders in the church. However, if they miss it and go on and you are an elder in that body, it may be that you should stand up and wait to be recognized by the leader. Then speaking in love, not in an argumentative manner, not in an attitude of being more holy, not in a dogmatic manner, you should say something like this:

"According to the apostle Paul, when a prophecy is given it's to be judged. 1 Corinthians 14:29 says, **Two or three prophets should speak, and the others should weigh carefully what is said.** I've weighed this message carefully and I don't feel it was from God." You might continue, "The words I heard," quote them to the best of your ability, "are contrary to my understanding of the scripture where it says... Pastor, at this point, I leave it in your hands."

Always turn the attention of the people back to the leader. By your words, recognize his authority and try not to leave an opening for another to jump up and argue with what has been said.

If the message was in tongues and you felt a condemning spirit, an evil spirit, a spirit of depression, or any other spirit coming on the body of Christ, stand up and say so. That is one of the responsibilities of leadership.

If you aren't in a position of responsibility in that body and you know a message isn't from God, you can bind the spirit in operation and then stop – in the spirit – any ill effects from that message. Following that, you should go to the pastor in private and tell him how you felt at the time.

That is what I did in the church where I knew from God that the visiting pastor was operating in lust demons. I bound those demon spirits during that service and then I talked to the pastor, privately, and told him what I knew in the spirit.

The pastor has a right to agree with you, or not to agree with you. You don't have a right to become offended about it! When I was telling the pastor about this man, I knew they were personal friends. I said, "Pastor, I'm going to tell you what I know, and I don't want you to say anything because you haven't had time to pray about it. You don't know if you disagree with me or not, and I'm not going to have my feelings hurt either way. God did say I was to tell you and I'm going to obey."

I told him what I saw and then I said, "Oh, there is one more thing, God said just now that I was to tell you this for your protection and the protection of the church. Now as far as I'm concerned that's the end of it."

I didn't ask him if he agreed with me! When you go to the pastor or the leader of a meeting, and your feelings are hurt because that person doesn't accept what you say immediately, that may be an indication that you weren't operating in the Spirit.

Now, what if another person came to the leader and shared the same thing? That is God's plan. Not just one person operating in distinguishing between spirits, but every believer. Then, false leaders would be afraid to come around. The believers living in sin and deceived by Satan into thinking God doesn't care, would straighten out their lives.

Paul wrote to the Corinthians, **Every matter must be established by the testimony of two or three witnesses (2 Corinthians 13:1).**

Satan's Devices

God says we're not to be ignorant about the spirits around us – the spirits that are involved in our businesses – in our friends – the spirits that exist around us. We cannot just think something is right, we must confirm it in our own spirit. Paul wrote, **...for we are not unaware of his schemes (2 Corinthians 2:11).** He also wrote, **those who are led by the Spirit of God are the sons of God (Romans 8:14).**

A lady was invited to speak at a large church across town from where we were living some time ago. When we were told she was coming, we felt some concern but didn't spend time praying about it. It wasn't our church home. We wouldn't be there. We thought it didn't make any difference in our lives.

Early the next morning while I was working at my desk, not consciously thinking about this lady or her "ministry," God started showing me the nature of the spirit of this woman by the operation of the revelation gifts. He showed me that the people she was laying her hands on were receiving curses. I knew from God that she was a powerful, very evil witch.

I went into A.L.'s office and shared with him what the Lord had shown me. He listened to me, but God hadn't spoken to him about this lady. He didn't feel the intensity I did. He asked, "Why are you so upset about this? How does it concern us?"

About that time, the door-bell rang and it was a friend who was very upset. She came in exclaiming, "I'm sorry to come so early, but I've got to talk to you!" She continued, "I was praying this morning and this is what the Lord showed me." She started sharing with us, almost word for word, what I had just told A.L. about this "guest speaker" being a witch.

God had spoken it to me and then confirmed it through a friend because His desire was for us to come against it in the spirit. The three of us sat in the comfortable surroundings of our living room and began a confrontation with a witch somewhere across town.

A.L. started praying, "God, you didn't show us this, You didn't bring our friend here to confirm what Joyce knew, without there being a reason. Lord, show us exactly what to do." In a few minutes, we had complete authority to bind those fortune-telling spirits and familiar spirits, and we did. We continued in warfare until I saw, in the spirit, angels surrounding the platform of that church. They were standing with their backs to the platform, their hands joined, facing the audience, as the witch stood on the platform. We knew we had won the victory in the spirit realm and we went on about our day's work. We heard later that as she stood on that platform with thousands watching, none of the "usual manifestations" occurred.

The pastor asked the same lady back again a few months later and God wouldn't allow us to do a thing! Day after day, we would ask the Lord if we could bind those spirits but we couldn't. God didn't allow us to operate in that area. Finally, the night she was speaking, we asked the Lord why we could do nothing. He replied, "It's not yours to do. A decision has been made." The second time she was invited, God didn't allow us to intervene.

This lady went on "ministering" in that church and others for many years. She laid her hands on leader after leader in these churches and we knew she was placing curses on them. When someone would ask, we would warn them about her. Many would tell us about her meetings and how "spiritual" she was. Finally, we learned that another minister videotaped her "ministering" with a telescopic lens and proved that many of the physical signs and wonders she was producing were trickery. He sent copies of it to many ministries around the United States and her involvement with the churches was finally stopped.

This is just one example of why we cannot be ignorant of Satan and his devices.

To Bind or Cast Out

When someone comes into a service with an evil spirit, you don't have authority to cast it out unless the person gives you that authority. Possessing, or not possessing, that spirit is that individual's choice, not yours.

In a recent meeting, a man walked up to A.L. and me. He asked, "What do you think about this belt buckle?" He was wearing a beautiful silver buckle on his belt.

Something must have been bothering him about it or he wouldn't have asked. I replied, "I don't know. I don't see anything." Then I stopped and we began to pray in the Spirit. I reached over and put my finger tips against that buckle as we continued to pray a few seconds more. I took my fingers away from the buckle and said, "Well, if it were mine, I would never wear it again."

Then as I looked back at that belt buckle, just glanced at it, I saw right in the center of the buckle a tiny, silver face with tiny ears, with a tongue sticking out at me. I looked at A.L. and said, "Do you see that?" "Yes," he replied. We had looked at it closely before and there was no design like that. We looked at it a few minutes later and we didn't see it. The demon had manifested himself as I had touched the belt while we prayed in the Spirit.

The man said, "I'm going to destroy it! I'll never wear it again." That's an obvious discerning of spirits!

Chapter Ten

Responsibilities of Leadership

The Courage of Early Believers

Leaders today must have the courage of Peter. There was a great revival in Samaria and a certain man had a marvelous conversion story. He had been a sorcerer, and everyone in that city knew him. He accepted Jesus as his Savior and was baptized. In our modern way of thinking, his testimony could win thousands to the Lord. We could reason that God could use his testimony and influence to reach many others – but the man was still in sin. This story is found in the eighth chapter of the book of Acts.

Now for some time a man named Simon had practiced sorcery in the city and amazed all the people of Samaria. He boasted that he was someone great, and all the people, both high and low, gave him their attention and exclaimed, 'This man is the divine power known as the Great Power.' They followed him because he had amazed them for a long time with his magic.

But when they believed Philip as he preached the good news of the kingdom of God and the name of Jesus Christ, they were baptized, both men and women. Simon himself believed and was baptized. And he followed Philip everywhere, astonished by the great signs and miracles he saw.

When the apostles in Jerusalem heard that Samaria had accepted the Word of God, they sent Peter and John to them. When they arrived, they prayed for them that they might receive the Holy Spirit, because the Holy Spirit had not yet come upon any of them; they had simply been baptized into the name of the Lord Jesus. Then Peter and John placed their hands on them, and they received the Holy Spirit.

When Simon saw that the Spirit was given at the laying on of the apostles' hands, he offered them money and said, 'Give me also this ability so that everyone on whom I lay my hands may receive the Holy Spirit' (Acts 8:9-19).

We might have excused his request. After all, how could he have known it was wrong? We would all understand that he was a "baby Christian." Perhaps someone could have taken him aside privately and taught him more of the Word. What did the courageous leaders of that time do?

Peter answered, 'May your money perish with you, because you thought you could buy the gift of God with money! You have no part or share in this ministry, because your heart is not right before God. Repent of this wickedness and pray to the Lord. Perhaps he will forgive you for having such a thought in your heart. For I see that you are full of bitterness and captive to sin' (Acts 8:20-23).

Peter knew the thoughts of the man's heart. He discerned the man's spirit and he addressed sin as sin. Because Peter did this, Simon was given the opportunity to repent.

101

God is looking for leaders as courageous as the apostle Paul. The apostle Paul wasn't afraid to put blindness on a man who was opposing God. We have this account in Acts 13:8-12.

But Elymas the sorcerer (for that is what his name means). opposed them and tried to turn the proconsul from the faith. Then Saul, who was also called Paul, filled with the Holy Spirit, looked straight at Elymas and said, 'You are a child of the devil and an enemy of everything that is right! You are full of all kinds of deceit and trickery. Will you never stop perverting the right ways of the Lord? Now the hand of the Lord is against you. You are going to be blind, and for a time you will be unable to see the light of the sun.'

Immediately mist and darkness came over him, and he groped about, seeking someone to lead him by the hand. When the proconsul saw what had happened, he believed, for he was amazed at the teaching about the Lord.

Paul was bold and as a result, the proconsul believed in Jesus.

Confrontation Can Bring Repentance

Years ago, I was managing a Christian bookstore located in a large church. We were open before and after the various services and the store would be packed with hundreds of people. Several people in the church worked in the store during these rush times as volunteers.

An attractive lady came to me one Sunday morning. She said she was new in the church and wondered if it would be possible to become a volunteer in the bookstore. This would give her

102

an opportunity to become a part of the church and to become better acquainted with the people. I talked to her for a few minutes about her experience in selling and making change and agreed it would be good for both of us. She was to start that evening.

While we were at lunch, A.L. asked why the lady was in my office. I told him that she was beginning that evening as a volunteer. A.L. said, "Joyce, that's the lady who's having an affair with the married man I've been counseling. He moved here from Tennessee trying to get away from her. She followed him here and even to this church."

What should I do? Should I allow her to work in the store and thus seem to condone the way she was living? Should I make some excuse that we really didn't need another volunteer? Should I just say nothing and "let the Lord work it out"?

Believe me, I wanted "to let the Lord work it out!" And God did have a definite plan, but to my despair, it included me. I prayed all Sunday afternoon. I asked God not to let her ever show up again. I questioned why her sinful life style should involve me.

When she came into the store that evening, I took her back into my office. I told her that I hadn't been aware of the sin she was living in when I had talked to her that morning. I called adultery, sin. I didn't refer to it as a "situation" or some other compromising word. As I talked to her about what she was doing and about God's viewpoint so plainly expressed in His Word, tears began flowing down my face. I hurt for her so much I could hardly stand it. That conversation was one of the hardest things I've ever done in my life! At first, the lady tried to explain away the sin. "God knew it was different for her. I just didn't understand the special circumstances..." She became more and more angry and finally stormed out of my office.

I went over that conversation again and again in my mind. How could I have been more kind? Had I spoken the Word of God in love? Why hadn't I known there was sin when I first talked to her? Why hadn't I distinguished that sinful spirit? How had I missed God?

About a year after this happened, I had resigned from the church staff and was in the store for the last time. A lady waited until the store was empty and then came up to me. "You don't remember me, do you?" she asked. Instantly I knew it was this same lady. I smiled, hesitantly, and said, "Yes, I do."

She began to tell me how mad she was at me and at the church that night. She had left my office, stormed out to her car and started home. She told God just how terrible I was, how little love and understanding I had. Then God spoke to her. "She told you the exact truth! You are living in sin!" And suddenly, she saw herself as God saw her. She recognized her sin and asked God for His forgiveness. She immediately moved to another state.

A year later, God sent her back to encourage me! The first conversation was hard. The second one was joyous. I had wondered many times why I missed knowing there was sin in her life when I first talked to her, but God knew that if He had told me then, I would never have been forced into the conversation where I had confronted her with her sin. That was His plan.

One evening, A.L. and I were talking with a pastor in Chicago whom we knew very casually. He asked about an international ministry located in California under which he was considering putting his church. As he asked the question, God said, "The seeds of destruction are already in place." I said to the pastor, "I don't know them. All that I've heard about them is good, but as you asked the question, God said, 'The seeds of destruction are already in place.'" I didn't expand on that. I didn't surmise what the seeds might be. I said the exact words I heard and left it at that.

Months later, we were given a cassette tape and the speaker was the head of this international ministry. As we listened to his message, my spirit was gladdened! He spoke of the wonderful growth of his ministry and how he had marveled that God could and did let it grow as it had. He told how he had felt so inadequate when he was pushed into a place of leadership. Then he spoke of how this feeling of inadequacy had caused him to ignore his responsibilities. He had ignored sin in the lives of those under him. He had played the part of "Mister Nice Guy." Then God spoke to him through a prophet and said total destruction was coming if he didn't deal with sin as sin. He went on to tell of the hard times in his ministry as he had rooted out the sin. The sin wasn't in his life, but in the lives of those under him in the ministry. He had accepted his responsibility. He had removed the "seeds of destruction" from his ministry and the ministry has gone on in greater power.

Chapter Eleven

In Conclusion

Sometimes, we wonder why God doesn't just destroy the deceit around us. Why did He tell us there would be false apostles, false prophets, false ministries as well as all the forces of evil around us?

Jesus gave us the answer. Jesus told them another parable: 'The kingdom of heaven is like a man who sowed good seed in his field. But while everyone was sleeping, his enemy came and sowed weeds among the wheat, and went away. When the wheat sprouted and formed heads, then the weeds also appeared.

The owner's servants came to him and said, 'Sir, didn't you sow good seed in your field? Where then did the weeds come from?'

'An enemy did this,' he replied.

The servants asked him, 'Do you want us to go and pull them up?'

'No,' he answered, 'because while you are pulling the weeds, you may root up the wheat with them. Let both grow together until the harvest. At that time I will tell the harvesters: First collect the weeds and tie them in bundles to be burned; then gather the wheat and bring it into my barn.'

He told them another parable: 'The kingdom of heaven is like a mustard seed, which a man took and planted in his field. Though it is the smallest of all your seeds, yet when it grows, it is the largest of garden plants and becomes a

107

tree, so that the birds of the air come and perch in its branches' (Matthew 13:24-32).

Jesus said the kingdom of God is like a field of wheat and tares and like a mustard tree.

In the parable of the wheat and tares, it's clear that Jesus was the sower of the good seed. Then Satan, the enemy, came along and sowed bad seeds, and both the wheat and the tares grew together. I understand that when tares are young, they look just like wheat. It's not until harvest time, when the head of the wheat is full, that the lack of good fruit becomes obvious and the tares can be recognized.

In the past, there have been some individuals and ministries who have looked good and seemed wonderful, but over a period of time, it has become apparent that their fruits were not good. These individuals and ministries have fallen into disrepute and disappeared.

I know we're the wheat, but I think we're also the servants. The servants asked him, "Do you want us to go and pull up the tares?" Sometimes, we want to pull up the tares. But Jesus knew the servants would make mistakes, that they wouldn't know some of the wheat from the tares.

We exist in a spiritual kingdom where there are both wheat and tares, but God hasn't left us defenseless. He has given us the gift of distinguishing between spirits. We can tell the "wheat" from the "tares" by hearing the voice of God in any situation and by knowing the fruits of people's lives.

Jesus explained this parable later to the disciples. He answered, 'The one who sowed the good seed is the Son of Man. The field is the world, and the good seed stands for the sons of the kingdom. The weeds are the sons of the evil one, and the enemy who sows them is the devil. The harvest is the end of the age, and the harvesters are angels. 'As the weeds are pulled up and burned in the fire, so it will be at the end of the age. The Son of Man will send out his angels, and they will weed out of his kingdom everything that causes sin and all who do evil. They will throw them into the fiery furnace, where there will be weeping and gnashing of teeth. Then the righteous will shine like the sun in the kingdom of their Father. He who has ears, let him hear' (Matthew 13:37-43).

The next thing that Jesus told us about the kingdom of God is that it's like the tiny mustard seed that can grow into a tree. Whenever I think of a spiritual tree, I think of the first Psalm of David. In that Psalm, we find a goal for our whole lifetime.

Blessed is the man who does not walk in the counsel of the wicked or stand in the way of sinners or sit in the seat of mockers. But his delight is in the law of the Lord, and on his law he meditates day and night. He is like a tree planted by streams of water, which yields its fruit in season and whose leaf does not wither. Whatever he does prospers.

Not so the wicked! They are like chaff that the wind blows away. Therefore the wicked will not stand in the judgment, nor sinners in the assembly of the righteous.

For the Lord watches over the way of the righteous, but the way of the wicked will perish (Psalms 1:1-6).

We are not to walk in the counsel of the wicked. We are to know the spirits of those from whom we receive. We are not to stand along the way with sinners. We must come out and be separate. We must leave "mixture" situations. We are not to sit with the mockers. When we first begin to operate in distinguishing between spirits, this can be a real temptation. However, the minute a mocking spirit or a spirit of pride begins to take root in us, we're in deception. We become the ones God is warning others about! We mustn't remain in the seat of the scornful.

Instead our delight, our protection from self-deception, our protection from evil, is staying in the Word of God. We aren't to meditate on the evil that is around us. We are to meditate on His Word day and night.

Then we can be like the tree of God planted by the stream, giving our fruit in season, with leaves that don't wither. Then all that we do shall prosper!